# INTRODUCTION

My food heroes have always been Elizabeth David and Keith Floyd. Kindred spirits I've always thought. Their cooking and writing is racy, naughty sometimes, but ultimately a joyful description of the appreciation of cooking as a way of life.

I grew up in Barming, a small village in Kent miles from the nearest shop, surrounded by hop fields and apple orchards. In those days, fresh produce was just that: seasonal and fresh. If my mother wanted tomatoes out of season then she used tinned tomatoes, if she needed peas, she used dried peas. This wasn't very long ago, but I grew up with an awareness of the seasons. I firmly believe in buying food in season and if possible from local suppliers. It just tastes so much better, no argument!

I hope this book will inspire you to cook, for your friends and family, but ultimately for yourself. Cooking is fun and exciting, from the first step of shopping for the ingredients, to trying new things in your kitchen, failing sometimes but trying again. And again. Because that is how you learn to cook and to cook well. I have no formal training, perhaps I'm lucky that I seem to be an instinctive cook. I know my years in Devon helping Keith Floyd on food shoots were the most instructional years of my life. Keith is a stickler for good honest ingredients, he insisted on integrity and authenticity in food, and that rubbed off on me.

My local market is cheaper and has a greater variety of fresh produce than the local superstore. If you can build a relationship with shopkeepers and stallholders, they will point you towards what is good and fresh. And it is worth the effort to seek out a good butcher and a good fishmonger.

Most of them are passionate about their trade, and when they realise you share their enthusiasm they will be your friend for life. Food is too personal to be left to the internet home delivery system! We live in a time when increasing numbers of people eat out, or buy ready-meals or take aways, and despite the proliferation of shiny kitchen ranges that would look more at home in a restaurant kitchen, and despite the heroic status of some of our TV chefs, cooking as an everyday pursuit is in decline.

Some of my friends are horrified at my basic cooking equipment. But good cooking is less about the equipment and more about the ingredients and the willingness to take risks. And maybe Bob Dylan on the stereo. Life doesn't have to be complicated, my favourite place to cook is on a beach with two gas rings!

I firmly believe you are what you eat. Our history and culture are defined by the food we eat and have eaten over the centuries. Recipes are handed down from generation to generation on scraps of paper or by word of mouth. Most of the recipes in this book are tried and tested traditional British standards, I've given them a personal twist here and there, because that is what cooking is all about. Recipes evolve and adapt to changing times and cooks, but the best are the simplest that have been taken just a little bit further.

To me food and cooking has always been about love, the love of the food I will cook, and the love for those I cook for. Meals are memorable not just for the good food but for the good company.

I believe that to cook a meal for someone is the highest compliment you can pay them.

*Clarissa Porter*

Published by
**KELSEY PUBLISHING LTD**
Printed by William Gibbons Ltd.
on behalf of
Kelsey Publishing Ltd, Cudham Tithe Barn, Berry's Hill, Cudham, Kent TN16 3AG.
Tel: 01959 541444   Fax: 01959 541400
E-mail: kelseybooks@kelsey.co.uk
Website: www.kelsey.co.uk
2007
**ISBN: 978 1 873098 85 1**

Spring

# Pulling mussels from a shell

*Clarissa Porter* takes us through the history of mussels and serves up some wonderful recipes

In 1235 an Irishman named Patrick Walton was shipwrecked on the coast of Brittany. He hung nets from poles in the sea in an attempt to catch sea birds, but he was surprised to find the poles became covered in mussels! From that moment nearly 800 years ago comes the 'farming' of mussels today. Poles and ropes are hung in the sea and mussels attach themselves to the ropes and poles. The area Patrick Walton was shipwrecked is still a primary producer of mussels caught this way. Mussels from here are called 'Moules Bouchots', bouchot means wooden pole I believe.

Mussels have been eaten in these islands since time began, almost. In archaeological digs, mussel shells have been found in human settlements dating back over 6,000 years. Sites of Roman villas are littered with oyster and mussel shells.

These were mostly freshwater mussels. The rivers of Britain teemed with mussels. They were not only a source of good nutritious food, some contained pearls! In the Middle

**Famous fish chef Keith Floyd**

Ages pearls from mussels were used as ornamentation on the clothing of Kings and Queens. This reached its peak during the reign of Queen Elizabeth. If you visit the National Portrait Gallery, or any of the great stately homes, such as Burghley House, you can stand in front of contemporary portraits of Elizabeth and marvel at the possibly thousands of pearls sewn onto her extraordinary dresses and into her hair ornaments. I've looked at these pictures many times over the years, wondering at the workmanship displayed on the dresses, but only recently did I discover the pearls came from humble mussels found in British rivers. One of the earliest written recipes for mussels is in a book called 'The Queen-Like Closet' by Elizabeth Woolley, published in 1672. This describes mussels parboiled in their own liquor, dried and floured, fried and then put into a pot with red wine, anchovy and allspice, and stewed together. Not much has changed since then.

Unfortunately with the coming of the Industrial Revolution, pollution began to kill off the freshwater mussel stocks. The life cycle of

# Norfolk mussel trenchers

This is a wonderfully old and rustic dish, and there's no washing up! A trencher was originally a hard crust of pastry which was used as a plate.

Serves 4

**4 pints of cleaned mussels (2kg cleaned mussels, a pint is about 440g)**
**3 shallots, chopped**
**150ml (¼ pint) white wine**
**handful of fresh parsley, chopped**
**3 cloves of garlic, crushed**
**50g (2oz) butter, softened**
**4 doorsteps of thick white country bread**
**Thyme or parsley to garnish**

For the sauce
**50g (2oz) butter**
**50g (2oz) plain flour**
**450ml (16fl oz) milk**
**salt and pepper**

### METHOD
Place the shallots, parsley and wine in a saucepan with the cleaned mussels. Cook for about 5 minutes until the mussels have opened. Discard any that remain closed. Drain the mussels through a colander set over a bowl so as to save the liquor. Allow the mussels to cool. When cool, shuck the mussels from their shells and set aside.

Preheat your oven to 190oC (375oF, gas 5). Blend together some chopped parsley, butter, and the crushed garlic.

Spread this mixture on both sides of the bread slices. Place each slice in an individual oven dish. Bake in the oven for 10 to 15 minutes turning once. While the bread is in the oven, make the sauce by melting the butter and stirring in the flour. After a few minutes, remove from the heat and gradually add the milk until you have a smooth sauce. Now add the mussels and the reserved liquor to this mixture, and warm through. Divide the mussels and the sauce equally between the 4 slices of bread, and return them to the oven for another 20 minutes.

Serve garnished with more parsley. I think you may need a fork!

# Mussels on a plank

Next, a dish inspired by the oldest method for cooking mussels and other shellfish. Thousands of years ago, our hunter, gatherer forefathers would have cooked their mussels by just putting them in the embers of a fire, and roasting them. This is still a good method, and ideal for a Spring picnic on a chilly beach. I don't recommend you try this at home, not indoors anyway! Definitely one for the boys, they seem to like playing with fire.

**3kg cleaned mussels**
**bottle of wine**
**Bread**
**Butter**
**1 plank**
**some pine twigs**

**METHOD**

Place your plank on a reasonably level surface. Arrange the mussels into three groups. Make circular rosette type patterns with the mussels. The mussels must be hinge side up.

Cover the mussels with pine needles and twigs, you need a pile about 25 to 30cms (10-12ins) high, so quite a lot! Set the twigs alight. Stand back. Butter the bread and open the wine. Allow the flames to die down, blow away the ash.

The mussels should have opened and hopefully they will have flipped over in the process. If any haven't opened you can try again, but after a second try if they haven't opened, throw them away!

This recipe is fun and you can reconnect with your inner prehistoric self!

**John Noakes eating mussels in Majorca**

the freshwater mussel can be 100 years, so once the cycle is damaged or interrupted it is almost impossible to revive. Recently, surviving stocks have been decimated by indiscriminate pearl hunting. Freshwater mussels are designated 'endangered' and it is illegal to fish for them, rivers are patrolled and protected in an effort to revive stocks of this poor little mollusc. Now in the entire country, mussels are only to be found in 22 rivers, and they are only breeding in one river. Mussels cannot breed unless they are part of a large 'bed', they need to be very close to each other to successfully breed, because they don't travel. Even if a mussel reproduces, 95% of the young mussels die before they reach sexual maturity and can in turn begin to breed.

Sadly, I don't think we will ever be eating freshwater mussels again in this country. Thankfully we still have saltwater mussels, which are being commercially produced all over the world. I would favour mussels from Scotland and the Shetlands over most of the other producing areas. And a word of warning: picking mussels from a beach to eat should be treated with caution.

If you want to collect mussels for food, ask your local Council if there are any current warning notices in operation. The sea around the British Isles is regularly checked for contamination, and though it is mostly OK, sometimes warnings are issued. If you live near the coast you may have seen notices displayed sometimes regarding the dangers of eating shellfish gathered from the shore. Mussels feed by filtering water, and if there is any harmful bacteria present they will collect it. Better safe than sorry!

For many people in this country, their introduction to mussels will have been the seaside seafood kiosk, and a tub of vinegary mussels eaten with your fingers. When I was young, most pubs had a seafood stall at weekends selling shellfish and jellied eels.

My own introduction to mussels came one night in the East End of London. All of the menfolk in my mother's family were 'in the print'. One night when I was very small I was taken to the *Daily Mirror* printing works

underground in Holborn to watch the machines start up and produce the next day's papers, a tremendously deafening, but as it turned out, formative experience. After the first editions came off the presses and were tied in bundles, they were tossed into the backs of a stream of waiting vans, which roared off into the night. At some point someone suggested I go in one of the vans. This was really exciting, like taking part in some sort of Grand Prix, the vans had sliding doors in the front which were always open! The driver stopped only long enough to toss a pile of newspapers into a shop doorway before tearing away again. Suddenly we stopped at a seafood stall, the legendary Tubby Isaac's in Whitechapel. It was the early hours of the morning, but the place was crowded with other van drivers, cabbies, and the sort of East End life you see in films!

I tasted my first mussels that night, and I've been hooked ever since, though these days I prefer to cook them in their shells and eat them in the comfort of home, preferably with a group of friends. They make for an excellent friendly meal, cheap and very easy to prepare. I love the sound of the shells clicking in the bowl as you reach in, and I love using the discarded shells as spoons to scoop out another succulent mussel. Some of my most memorable meals have been involved mussels. I have cooked and eaten mussels with Keith Floyd in Kinsale, and in Majorca I was taken by John Noakes and his wife to a tiny cafe on a beach that could only be reached by boat. We sat around a large communal bowl of mussels washed down with red wine watching the Mediterranean lap gently at our feet. In the last few years Moules Marinieres has become ubiquitous in trendy restaurants and pubs, reminding us of hot lazy holidays in France or Spain.

But this isn't some exotic foreign dish, imagine Roman soldiers guarding Hadrian's Wall in the long British winter, they could have been eating mussel and onion stew. 'Mussel Stew' doesn't sound nearly so romantic as Moules Marinieres, but it is basically the same dish! Musselburgh near Edinburgh has the Romans to thank for its name. They invaded Scotland in AD80 and built a fort and then a bridge at the mouth of the River Esk. In the process they discovered extensive mussel beds.

The town grew around Mussel fishing and was called Mussel Town. Today, Musselburgh's coat of arms consists of 3 mussels and 3 anchors. Buying mussels these days is simplicity itself. It is possible to buy ready cleaned mussels, but if you buy them only partially cleaned put them in a bowl of clean water. Remove the 'beard', this is the tuft of hair like filaments that the mussels use to attach themselves to a rope or post. Throw away any that are damaged or cracked. If any are open give them a sharp tap. If they don't close when you tap them, throw them away.

Then drain and repeat the process. Don't leave them in the freshwater too long. When they are cooked, they will open. Throw away any that refuse to open after the cooking process. Strictly speaking, March and April are the beginning of the end of the mussel season, until September. But the reality is that these days mussels are available year-round. ●

# Mussels steamed in ale

When you ask 'What Did The Romans Do For Us?' Well they celebrated our mussels for a start! This recipe is for me is the closest to the Roman method for cooking mussels.

**2.5kg cleaned mussels**
**8 cloves of garlic, finely chopped**
**3 shallots**
**handful of fresh parsley**
**1 sprig of thyme**
**1 bay leaf**
**Tarragon, sprig or two**
**2 pints of ale (not lager!)**
**150ml (¼ pint) of cream**
**pepper**
**METHOD**
Put the cleaned mussels in a very large pan, season with pepper. Pour on the ale, and everything else except the cream. Cover and cook for 8 to 10 minutes on a high heat, until the mussels have opened. Discard any that remain closed. Add the cream and cook for a further 3 to 4 minutes.

Remove the herb sprigs and serve the mussels in a large bowl with lots of bread to sop up the juices.

Who needs Moules Mariniere? Not me!

# Stuffed mussels

Another well remembered dish, a classic and simple recipe. Try and search out slightly larger mussels than normal. Even people that are a bit iffy about eating mussels because of their appearance or their seaside smell can be converted by this recipe. The crispy bread crumb and garlic butter makes this a good introduction to mussels for children. You can easily adapt and change it to your own taste, try them with a little chilli or with a little cheese or orange zest. This dish makes either an excellent starter, or a main course in its own right. Experiment, have fun!

**12 cleaned mussels per person**
**50ml (2fl oz) water**
**1 clove of garlic**
**1 shallot**
**1 handful of parsley**
**Zest of 1 lemon**
**100g (4oz) fresh breadcrumbs**
**salt and pepper**

**METHOD**
Place the mussels in a large pan containing about 1cm (½in) of boiling water. Cover and cook for about 3 minutes. The mussels should have opened. Drain through a colander and discard any that haven't opened or are broken. Save the drained liquor, you can use it to make fish stock.

Pre-heat your grill to a high heat. Put the butter, parsley, lemon zest and garlic into a small blender, or chop by hand till you have a coarse texture mixture. Remove one half of each mussel shell. Arrange the mussels on a baking sheet. Put a dot of the garlic butter you have prepared onto each mussel, and cover with a sprinkle of breadcrumbs. Grill for about 3 minutes, until the breadcrumbs are golden.

Serve at once.

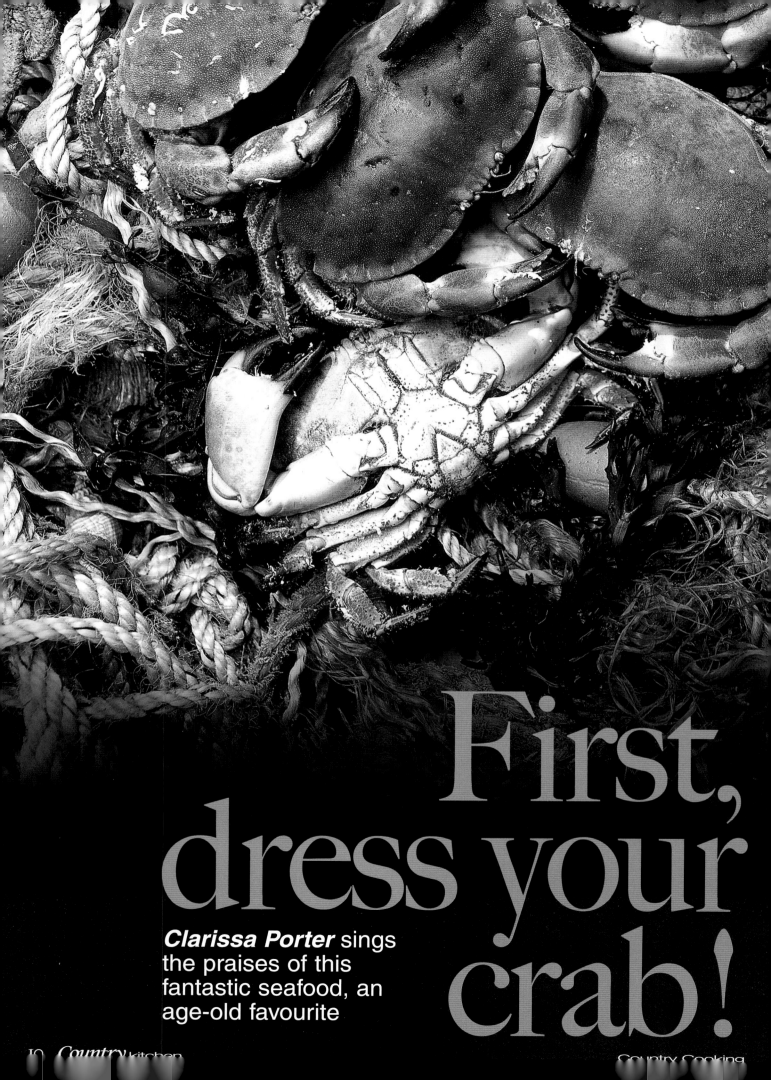

# First, dress your crab!

**Clarissa Porter** sings the praises of this fantastic seafood, an age-old favourite

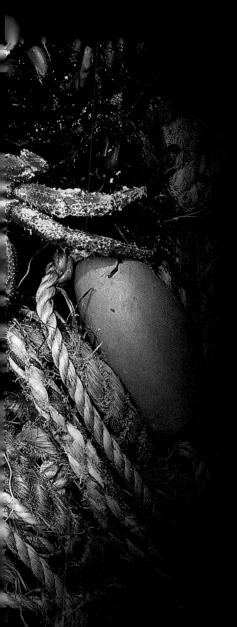

When I was young, summer holidays sooner or later involved dangling my legs over the edge of a pier or jetty with a crab line, trying to catch crabs (and secretly hoping I wouldn't). Of course, we only ever caught tiny green shore crabs, which we collected in buckets and then threw back. We children were carrying on a tradition of crabbing that goes back thousands of years in these islands. Evidence has been found that our prehistoric ancestors in Scotland and the Orkneys fished for crabs using woven baskets, similar to the crab pots used today.

But you'd be surprised how many people have never eaten crab. Like me, my friends have eaten 'crab sticks', and possibly, like me, they were brought up on a diet that included crab paste sandwiches, but the real thing? No! They gave a variety of excuses: too fiddly, too expensive, and just a bit too scary. What it really boiled down to was that they simply didn't know how to eat a crab, let alone cook one.

You see, crabs, like cockles and winkles, whelks and jellied eels, have become too difficult to handle in many people's eyes, and even a bit down market. But I shouldn't have been surprised. Some people think cooking and eating any seafood is far too complicated. When I enthuse about some fish dish I've eaten, the response is often only: 'does it have bones..?' I may be a fish-eating fanatic now but there was a time when I had never eaten a real crab, considering them an adventure too far.

What changed? Well, my perceptions. Healthy eating had become topical and trendy. I read that crabs were really good for you because they contain Selenium, Iodine, and Omega 3, in fact more Omega 3 than any other shellfish, apart from mussels. I also discovered that crab sticks weren't actually made from crabs, but were the burgers of the seafood world, made from all sorts of processed fish parts, which wasn't very appetising.

An evening out at a local Chinese restaurant saw me ordering baked crab. I could see my friends looking at each other in a 'she'll be sorry' sort of way. I had no idea what to expect, but then I tasted my first whole crab. It was really messy because it came swimming in some sauce, probably black bean. As I picked away decorously with my knife and fork, the owner came over laughing and told me to be bold, pick

# Baked crab (Partan pie)

Partan pie is a Scottish dish, partan being Gaelic for crab. Crab is also known as partan on the Isle of Man. I've read there used to be a saying 'Wha ca'ed ye partan-face?' which is a mildly insulting way of saying 'why is your face all screwed up like a crab?' It's probably something to do with the windy location. This recipe isn't a real pie of course, but it is very old and traditional. Originally it was cooked by heating a shovel and holding it over the crab!

Serves 1

**1 small crab (cooked) per person**
**Nutmeg**
**Juice of 1 lemon**
**Cayenne, a pinch**
**25g (1oz) melted butter**
**Salt and pepper**

For the topping:
**25g (1oz) bread crumbs**
**25g (1oz) melted butter**

## METHOD
Remove the meat from the shell, claws and so on. Put the meat into a bowl and reserve the shell. Mix the meat together with 25g (1oz) of the melted butter, and season with salt and pepper, adding a few scrapes of nutmeg. Add a pinch of cayenne and the lemon juice.

Return the meat mixture to the crab shell, cover with the bread crumbs, and spot with the other melted butter. Place under a hot grill until the breadcrumbs are crisp and golden. (Alternatively, place the crab on the ground and hold a red-hot shovel over it). Serve with dry white wine.

napkin around my neck and promised me a hot towel when I was finished. Since that night I haven't looked back, although I'm not sure I'd eat crab with quite so much sauce again, I don't want to mask the fantastic flavour!

Someone once said that 'eating good crab was God's gift to drycleaners'! This is very true. Crabs are perhaps the ultimate finger food if eaten whole when freshly cooked.

Now I eat crab whenever I can, either whole or dressed, cold or hot, in soup or as crab cakes.

## Snack shacks

Unfortunately, the opportunities for eating good crab in restaurants are limited in this country. If any of you have travelled in America, particularly near the coast, you will know of the abundance of Crab Shacks. One of my most memorable meals ever was at one such shack in the Florida Keys. It was literally a tiny wooden shack, open sides, wooden benches, great food but watch out for alligators in the car park!

This concept of unpretentious good seafood, served in similarly unpretentious surroundings at a reasonable price, is rare in this country but, as Bob Dylan said, 'the times they are a changing'.

Several times a year I make the trek to Mersea Island in Essex, to The Company Shed in West Mersea (tel: 01206 382700). The Shed is the brainchild of Country kitchen reader Heather Haward.

She and her husband Richard saw the seafood shacks in New England and thought they could combine their family business of oyster fishing with the type of laid-back, casual honesty of the shacks they saw in America. The Company Shed lies at the end of the road in West Mersea, next to the Lifeboat Station, surrounded by boats and boatyards. It is exactly what it says – a wooden shed, with a long fresh fish counter and tables crammed together, plastic table cloths, mismatched chairs, and friendly staff watched over by Caroline, Heather's daughter. You'll find Heather helping out at weekends, when the queue for a table stretches out of the door and down the street. I always seem to go on a Sunday, which is their busiest day even in the winter.

You can't book, just turn up, give your name, and they write it on a blackboard, and give you an idea of how long you're going to have to wait. Then you can stroll around the fishing boats and while away the minutes collecting oyster shells on the beach until it's your turn. You may have to share a table, but don't worry, everyone is really friendly, and ready to share with you.

Share what? I forgot to say, the Shed only serves fish, shellfish, and salad. You will have to take your own bread and drinks. Waiting for our table we sat at the back next to a stack of tanks, water cascading through, containing live crabs, and watched fascinated as customers arrived carrying baskets of extras: bread, wine, water, wet-wipes! (The Shed provides a roll of kitchen towel on each table.) Some people brought plastic bags so they could take home the remains of their meal, to make soup I expect.

Order at the counter and then enjoy a truly memorable, and cheap, meal. I had the Seafood platter: half a crab, Tiger prawns, prawns, shrimps, mussels, cockles, smoked mackerel, and smoked salmon. The couple sharing our table started with a Seafood platter each, and then went on to have plates of grilled mussels, and then scallops with bacon. They were still here when we left, thinking about what to order

# Fried crab with lime and herbs

This is definitely a 'fingers before forks' dish. After the previous traditional dish, Partan pie, here is one that is up to date and positively trendy. One to eat with friends – a lively gregarious meal, and messy. Have the wet wipes handy!

Serves 4

**1 freshly cooked crab, about 1.4kg (3lb 1oz)**
**4 eggs, beaten**
**A little cornflour**
**2 tbsp sesame oil**
**5 cloves of garlic, crushed**
**Fresh ginger, grated**
**Bunch of spring onions, cut into strips**
**2 tbsp dry sherry**
**1 tbsp soy sauce**
**1 tsp sugar**
**Juice of 1 lime**
**Small bunch of basil or coriander**

**METHOD**

Pull off the claws and the legs from the body and crack them. Dip the claws and the shell in beaten egg and then cornflour. Blanch the crab in boiling water for one or two minutes, and drain. Heat the oil in a large frying pan with a lid (or wok). Add the garlic and the ginger and fry for a few seconds. Then add everything else except the lime juice and the basil. Carefully add a little water, cover and cook for six to eight minutes on a medium heat, shaking the pan occasionally. Finally, squeeze over the lime juice and scatter torn basil or coriander.

Serve straight from the sizzling pan, or tip out onto a pretty serving dish. Encourage everyone to dive in!

Sunday lunch at the Shed, you'll never think about going to a pub for Sunday lunch again.

Thankfully, more and more places like this are opening up around the country. Here are a couple of suggestions: if you live on the Isle of Wight there is The Priory Oyster (www.priorybay.co.uk), and I have been to The Riverside Restaurant (tel: 01308 422011) in West Bay, Dorset. Cromer in Norfolk is famous for its crabs, but you'll have to be careful to avoid the more touristy-inclined establishments. Search out authentic Cromer crabs, and have a really simple treat, a Cromer crab sandwich.

## Buying the best crab

A few rules when buying crab: you can, of course, simply buy prepared crab meat, and for some of my recipes that is sufficient. But, assuming you are buying cooked fresh crab, always buy from a reputable source. Don't buy a crab with a cracked or broken shell, buy it from a refrigerated display or off ice. Use your normal food hygiene common sense, and keep raw food separate from cooked. It is a good idea to buy your shellfish last, and take it straight home and pop it in the fridge. Eat as soon as possible, as fresh as possible. You will need to allow 500g (1lb 2oz) per person, gross unprepared weight.

## Preparation

Really the only way to eat crab is freshly killed and cooked. If you're too squeamish to kill it yourself, buy from a fishmonger ask him to kill it for you. If you are going to cook from live, the best way is to use sea water if possible, with extra salt added, about a couple of tablespoons. Either put your crab in a freezer for at least two hours to render it comatose, and then plunge it into boiling water, or, put it into the cold water and gradually heat up to the boil. Allow to simmer – about 15 minutes for smaller crabs and 25 minutes for larger ones. Turn the heat off, and allow to cool.

To prepare the cooked crab for eating, twist off the claws and legs. Carefully insert the appointed knife to separate the hard top shell from the lower section where the legs were attached. Pull off the shell and remove the grey 'dead man's fingers' (the gills and so on). Scoop out the meat from the body and, using either special shop-bought skewers or a crochet hook, push and pull out every piece of meat from the claws and legs. You will probably have to use nutcrackers or special lobster crackers to break the claws. There will be brown meat from the main shell cavity, and white meat from the rest of the crab.

I think you can just serve the meat as it is with a salad, but if you want to 'dress' the crab, use the top shell as the 'bowl', add a squeeze of lemon to the brown meat and season to taste. Spoon into the middle of the shell. Mix some chopped parsley and maybe a scrape of nutmeg into the white meat. Some people add a chopped boiled egg but I like mine as simple as possible, and then spoon the white meat around the brown meat so that the shell is full. Serve with some salad, and oil and vinegar dressing. ●

# Cromer crab soup

This soup is as pretty as a spring garden. I love crab chowder with sweet corn, but this is a more visual feast. You might think that crab soup is a luxury dish, but crabs are not all that expensive. One large crab will easily make enough soup for four hungry people. You can substitute other vegetables if you wish.

Serves 4

**350g (12oz) fresh crab meat (from a cooked crab if possible)**
**25g (1oz) butter**
**2 sticks of celery, sliced lengthways**
**2 carrots, sliced**
**1 bunch of spring onions, sliced**
**1 courgette, sliced**
**900ml (1½ pints) chicken or fish stock (from a cube will do)**
**1 tsp tomato purée**
**45ml (2fl oz) dry sherry**
**Salt and pepper**

### METHOD

Melt the butter in a large saucepan and add the vegetables. Cover, and cook on a gentle heat till they soften but don't discolour. Stir in the tomato purée and then add the stock.

Simmer for 10 minutes. Remove from the heat. Add the sherry and season with salt and pepper. Add the crab meat. Place back on the heat and allow to heat through for another couple of minutes.

Serve garnished with chopped chives or the tops of spring onions.

# Crab cakes with garlic mayonnaise

Crab cakes come in all sorts of guises, and they are also a very historic way of preparing and eating crab. The earliest recipe I have found is dated 1685. These early recipes travelled to America with the Pilgrim Fathers and are now associated with New England.

Making a 'pattie' from either seafood or meat is one of the most ancient methods of preparing food known to us today. Crab cakes should be light and fluffy, and children will love them. They are a very good way of introducing children to crab. These days they are found in all the best restaurants and gastro pubs, so I suppose they have gained an air of sophistication far beyond their humble historic origins.

Serves 4

**350g (12oz) fresh crab meat (available at good fishmongers)**

**1 tbsp garlic mayonnaise (homemade)**
**2 tbsp Dijon mustard**
**2 tbsp parsley and chervil, chopped and combined**
**4 finely chopped spring onions**
**100g (4oz) dry breadcrumbs**
**Oil for frying or grilling**
**NB:** Make your breadcrumbs by whizzing stale bread in a blender to crumb, and then spread on a baking tray and place in an oven until they are golden

For the garlic mayonnaise:
**8 cloves of garlic, crushed**
**2 egg yolks**
**Juice of 1 lemon**
**450ml (16fl oz) oil, half virgin olive oil and half groundnut oil**
**Salt and pepper**
**Pinch of sugar (optional)**

## METHOD
To make the mayonnaise, place the crushed garlic in a bowl, add the eggs, stirring in gradually. Whisk gently and add the oil, drip by drip. Continue whisking until you have a thick golden mayonnaise. Season with the lemon, salt and pepper, and sugar if you think it needs it. Pour into a serving dish and keep cool.

To make the crab cakes, put your crab meat in a bowl, then add the egg, and one tablespoon of your homemade mayonnaise, add the Dijon mustard, herbs, spring onions, season with pepper and salt, and mix in the breadcrumbs. Divide the mixture into four. Shape into round patties about 20mm (¾in) thick. Shallow fry in a little oil until golden, or, brush with oil and grill, turning once. Serve with the rest of the garlic mayonnaise, lemon wedges and a green salad.

# Grow your cake and eat it!

**Clarissa Porter** meets a landscape gardener with a passion for making cakes, with a difference

**M**arch means the start of spring and the serious gardening season. For landscape gardener and amateur cook James Hazelrigg-Kinlay it means looking ahead to all the possibilities that the garden offers to his baking.

Born in South Africa, James discovered an aptitude for cooking when, as a small boy, he was denied the treat of fudge. He decided to cook his own, and so began a lifetime's interest in cooking in general and baking in particular.

His ambition was to be a garden designer, but South Africa was not the best place to study for this, so, in 1995, he came to England with wife Nicolette, to study Landscape Architecture and gain his diploma. They settled on the fringes of south London, near the banks of the River Quaggy. He set about rescuing the large neglected garden backing on to their Victorian house, while at the same time building up his successful garden design business.

For a while his cooking took a back seat. He travelled all over the country creating beautiful gardens and establishing his reputation as one of our foremost landscape architects. James worked long and hard developing his career but, following the birth of daughter Alice, he spent more time at home, rekindling his boyhood passion for cooking. For Alice's second birthday party he baked a very special cake, and suddenly found he was in demand from friends and local schools, to make cakes for parties and school fetes.

**James, daughter Alice and friend**

His interest reawakened, James read in a newspaper a recipe for a chocolate and beetroot cake, and realised he could combine both his interests and bake cakes using vegetables instead of the more usual ingredients. James started to hunt out recipes and found that wartime recipes were a good starting point. During those rationing years, cocoa was almost impossible to find, so beetroot was used as an alternative. Then a friend from the Bahamas gave him a recipe for baking with sweet potato,

and he was off, refining and practising his methods and techniques.

Today he still finds the time to bake cakes, and now he has help from seven-year-old Alice and her school friends. Most of his cakes are given to friends, and sometimes he barters them for something he needs. His cluttered but cosy kitchen is geared to cake making. There is a lingering smell of baking, and everywhere you look are piles of cake tins and moulds, and rows of enamel tins for flour and sugar, and heaps of the vegetables James uses to make his spectacular creations.

He grows his own vegetables, of course, and keeps chickens at the bottom of his garden. And in my book, anyone that keeps chickens in London is really rather special. I heard about James' cakes by word of mouth, and then I met him and Nicolette at a party two years ago. Now, whenever I need a cake for a special occasion I call on James. When he visits, bearing a cake, he can't tear his eyes off my garden; a passionate gleam appears in them, and I know he can see the garden I should have, rather than the embarrassing hodgepodge it is! Actually, I think he brings cakes as an excuse to stare out of my kitchen window and plan an assault on my garden, which he threatens to knock into shape.

He shared four of his favourite recipes with me. Please try them. I'm sure you'll be surprised and maybe inspired to experiment yourself with unusual ingredients.

James can be contacted by e-mail: jamesatgarden@hotmail.co.uk
or tel: 020 8297 0130.

# Carrot cake

Carrot cake recipes are older than you might think – the Oxford Dictionary of Food claims they have been used as sweeteners in cooking since the Middle Ages. Carrots as we know them today originated in Afghanistan in the Seventh Century; they contain more sugar than any other vegetable.

And it is a myth that they help you see in the dark – that was wartime propoganda to encourage us to eat more carrots!

375g (13oz) flour
2 tsp baking powder
2 tsp bicarbonate of soda
Pinch of salt
1 tsp cinnamon
375ml (13fl oz) sunflower oil
250g (9oz) caster sugar
4 free range eggs
3 medium carrots, grated
Handful of walnut pieces

**METHOD**

Mix together the oil, sugar, eggs, salt, and cinnamon. Sift the flour, baking powder and bicarb together, and fold in with the egg mixture. Then add the carrots – one coarsely grated and the other two finely grated – to the mixture. Then add the walnut pieces.

Put the mixture into a loose ring cake tin and place in a preheated oven at 150°C (300°F, gas 2) for about an hour. When it's ready a knife inserted into the cake should come out clean.

Ice with cream cheese icing (made from a small packet of cream cheese such as Philadelphia, sweetened to taste with icing sugar, and maybe a drop of vanilla essence or a scrape of orange zest). Decorate with whole walnuts.

# Courgette and lavender cake

This cake really brings the fragrance of a garden into your kitchen. James uses lavender oil (essence). He buys his lavender from Castle Farm in Shoreham, near Sevenoaks. They grow lavender and sell two types of oil for cooking, one for baking and one for other things, such as ice cream. They are five-times Gold Medal winners at Chelsea, so they must know a thing or two!

I can recommend a visit when the lavender fields are in bloom, they are spectacular. You can contact Castle Farm for advice or mail order at www.hopshop.co.uk or tel: 01959 523219.

If you are going to use your own lavender, or buy it elsewhere, please check that no chemicals have been used on the plants.

**225g (8oz) self-raising flour**
**125ml (4fl oz) sunflower oil**
**2 free range eggs**
**125g (4½oz) caster sugar**
**Pinch of salt**
**½ tsp baking powder**
**½ tsp bicarbonate of soda**
**1 large, or 2 small courgettes**
**9 drops of lavender essence (for baking)**
**Heads of about 10 lavender flowers**

## METHOD

Beat together the eggs, oil, and sugar. Add the salt and the lavender oil and flowers.

Then sift in the flour, baking powder and bicarb, and fold together. Grate the courgette into the mixture, and stir in. Put the mixture into two 20cm (8in) diameter sponge tins and bake for 30 minutes at 150°C (300°F, gas 2). Remove, make cream cheese frosting (as before, but no vanilla or orange essence), coloured with a drop of red and blue colouring (to make a lavender colour). Fill with the frosting and ice with the remainder. Decorate with a few stems of lavender.

"He realised he could combine both his interests and bake cakes using vegetables instead of the more usual ingredients.

# Chocolate and beetroot cake

During the War, chocolate and cocoa were in very short supply – the sweet ration was 350g (12oz) per person per month. The Ministry of Food issued leaflets and there was a daily radio broadcast from 'the kitchen front' advising of substitutes for unobtainable foods. Beetroot was considered a sweet alternative for chocolate, and leaflet number 40 gave a recipe for Beetroot pudding.

Luckily, we no longer have any trouble finding chocolate! And, equally fortunately, beetroots are officially the latest superfood, and we are advised to eat them regularly.

This cake is an excellent excuse to be healthy and eat chocolate at the same time!

300g (11oz) cooked and peeled beetroot
3 large eggs
80g (3oz) good cocoa (like Green and Blacks)
200ml (7fl oz) sunflower oil
Pinch of salt
200g (7oz) caster sugar
180g (6oz) flour
3 tsp baking powder

## METHOD

Mix the beetroot, eggs, sunflower oil, and salt together in a blender, tip into a bowl, then add the flour, sifting it in with the baking powder and the cocoa, and folding them all together.

Place the mixture in a greased, loose ring cake tin and bake in a preheated oven at 150°C (300°F, gas 2) for about 50 minutes, or until a knife comes out clean.

When cool, ice with chocolate icing (James used a proprietary pre-made chocolate fudge icing, the cheat!). Decorate with chocolate strands and silver balls.

# Simnel cake

What, is it Easter already? No! Simnel cakes were originally baked for Mothering Sunday. Another name for Mothering Sunday is Mid Lent Sunday, or Refreshment Sunday. The fourth Sunday in Lent was also known as Simnel Sunday – a day when the strict fasting rules of Lent were relaxed. Simnel cakes were given as appreciative gifts to Mothers. There is written evidence of this practise from the Seventeenth century, only more recently have Simnel cakes become associated with Easter. So it seems a good excuse to have Simnel cake twice!

James departs from the traditional appearance and cooks a delightfully modern eggy cake.

225g (8oz) flour
225 (8oz) butter
225g (8oz) caster sugar
55g (2oz) ground almonds
110g (4oz) glacé cherries
4 eggs, separated
225g (8oz) sultanas
110g (4oz) currants
25g (1oz) candied peel
Zest of 1 lemon
Pinch of salt
Pinch of baking powder

## METHOD

Grease a cake tin, about 20cm (8in) diameter. Sift together the flour, salt, and baking powder. Add the sugar to the butter and cream together, then add the lemon zest. Using just the egg yolks, beat them into your mixture. Fold in about half the flour and then whisk the egg whites until they are stiff and slowly fold them into the mixture. At the same time, add the remaining flour, and then the fruit and the peel.

Put the mixture into your tin and bake in a preheated oven for about two hours at 150°C (300°F, gas 2).

Remove, allow to cool and then make up some royal icing (icing sugar with egg white or water, or buy ready-made). Colour with a little food colour, ice your cake and decorate with tiny candy eggs.

# April Fool!

**Clarissa Porter** has some fun dishes to serve up on 1st April

**1**st April – the one day of the year when not only can you get away with playing harmless pranks on your friends and family but it's almost expected.

Although this custom is celebrated throughout the Western world, no one is sure of its origins. The Romans celebrated their New Year on or around this date, as do the Hindus. The Roman festival was called 'Hilaria', and was devoted to fun. Many other cultures had similar festivals around the beginning of April.

The Feast of the Annunciation was celebrated as the beginning of a New Year, so there is probably something about the change of the seasons that brought about this frivolous festival. In 1582 Pope Gregory replaced the old calendar, and New Year's Day moved to January 1st. Some people think that, understandably, the change was resisted, and those sticking to the old ways were treated as figures of fun. The French call this day 'Poisson d'Avril', or 'April Fish'. French children play pranks on each other by pinning pictures of fish onto their unsuspecting victims, and shouting 'Poisson d'Avril' If you watch The French Connection carefully, there is a scene in Marseilles where, in the background, children are pinning pictures of fish to each other. Originally they would have tried to pin dead fish onto their victims!

Some of the best April Fools' jokes have involved food. I can still remember seeing the TV report about the Spaghetti Harvest! Lots of people fell for that – maybe it was wishful thinking? Since the success of that spoof, radio, TV and newspapers have competed with varying degrees of success to trick us all on 1st April.

## Cook up a surprise

I thought it might be fun to cook some recipes that might surprise you, and amuse your children. Some may be familiar but, hopefully, others will be new and tempt you to try them.

The idea for this piece came from reading a passing reference to 'Northumberland Duck', and the accompanying observation that it wasn't duck at all, it was lamb.

I was intrigued and spent hours looking through cookery books and searching the internet, with no success other than a passing reference. I thought of contacting Clarissa Dickson Wright at her Cooks Bookshop in

# Sea pie (Scuttlebutt pie)

No fish involved here!

Sea pie was originally a very large pigeon pie. One of the recipes I have seen talks of needing 4lb of flour, 11/2lb pounds of butter, and 12 pigeons! Together with salt pork and three pints of water. So you can see how a pie like this could begin to feed large numbers of hungry seamen. I like the idea of sitting around a very large pie exchanging small talk. Sea pie is a corruption of the French word 'cipaille' which means layered meat pie. Not only is the meat layered, but layers of pastry are included, probably to stop the whole lot going overboard. Certainly the crust is more of a containing lid than a part of the dish. Here's my version for landlubbers. Yummy!

Serves 6+

**900g (2lb) pigeons, or another game bird, off the bone.**
**3 large potatoes, peeled and sliced**
**5 large flat mushrooms, peeled**
**1 large onion, sliced**
**450g (1lb) good bacon, salted if possible, thickly sliced**
**Chicken stock (make more than you will need, and keep it warm)**
**2 packets of shortcrust pastry**
**2 cloves mace, nutmeg, and allspice**

## METHOD

Having removed as many of the bones from your pigeons as possible, place in a bowl with the onions, cloves, pinch of mace and allspice, a scrape of nutmeg, and a little pepper. Put in a fridge and leave for about an hour. You will need a casserole dish about 22cm (9in) to 30cm (12in) diameter.

Roll out some of the pastry, and cut two circles of pastry the same diameter as the casserole dish. Then take slices of bacon and arrange on the bottom of the dish, covering the bottom. Now take about one third of the game meat and arrange on top of the bacon. Then take about one third of the potatoes and arrange on top of the meat. Next, arrange some of the mushrooms on top of the potatoes. Now take one of your circles of pastry and place on top of the layered ingredients, cutting a small hole in the middle. Next repeat all of the above! Two more layers, with pastry again between the middle and the top layers, and again cut a small hole in the middle of the pastry.

Finally, cut out a pastry lid for your pie, leaving a hole in the centre. Decorate the pie lid and glaze with egg wash. Push a metal skewer through the holes in the pastry, and then pour in the warm stock till it bubbles out of the top. Wait until it settles and top up. Loosely cover the top with greaseproof paper. Place in an oven, preheated to 200°C (400°F, gas 6) until you think the liquid is bubbling – about 45 minutes. Reduce the heat to 180°C (350°F, gas 4), and continue to cook for about 90 minutes. It's a very slow cooking process. About 30 minutes before the end, remove the greaseproof paper. Serve simply with a pint of beer!

Edinburgh. But a call to the number listed just produced a very grumpy Scotsman telling me that the book shop had closed down a long time ago. Then I sent off a barrage of e-mails, to lamb producers and EBLEX, (The English Beef and Lamb Executive), and to a site called Northumbrian Larder. Sadly, there was only one reply: Ian Bell of Gillgate Lamb in the Yorkshire Dales kindly told me he'd never heard of it, but wished me luck in my search. I had begun to think this was a mythic recipe – something that didn't really exist but was spoken of in hushed tones at dinner parties, a Holy Grail of the Foodie World.

Finally, I wrote to the Northumberland Gazette. The day it was published I received a 'phone call from someone called Dave Wardle and, yes, he knew of the recipe! He said he used to buy his meat from a high class butchers in Newcastle, and the butcher used to prepare lamb this way. The shop had long since closed. But, he had recently visited Wallington Hall near Cambo in Northumberland, where there was a farm shop. And who should be the manager? The butcher from Newcastle! Dave gave me the number, and I finally spoke to someone who knew about Northumberland Lamb.

So, perseverance does pay. And, although it turns out that the recipe is really just a way of presenting a lamb joint, I like it for its obscurity and authenticity. Far better than some of the April Fools' recipes I've seen which just consist of hiding candy in pies and colouring food.

Many of the recipes I researched have charming, misleading, or obscure names. Some are full of double meaning, but not in front of the children! Scotland and the North of England are a rich source for odd-sounding recipes: Singing Hinnies, Cullen Skink, and the most outrageous, Fitless Cock! Unfortunately, despite their strange names they are sometimes rather bland dishes. Fitless Cock is a type of dumpling cooked in a muslin bag. Some might say it resembles a chicken without feet, hence 'fitless' meaning 'footless'. Singing Hinnies are a type of currant scone, said to get their name from the noise they made cooking on a griddle, and Cullen Skink is a fish soup made with smoked haddock.

Interestingly, as most of these recipes are old and traditional, they usually have a story behind them, which I always find fascinating.

You may remember Gordon Ramsay cooking Christmas dinner for our troops in Afghanistan. One of the dishes he served was reported to be Scuttlebutt Pie, which was described as a naval dish. Another elusive recipe! I started looking for a recipe for Scuttlebutt Pie and, like Northumberland Duck, no one had the slightest idea what it was. I even asked old sailors but to no avail. 'Scuttlebutt' was the name given to a barrel placed on the deck of a warship, and from which sailors could help themselves to a drink of water. The original water cooler in fact, and sailors would stand around the Scuttlebutt gossiping. It is not a word we use in this country, but in America it is part of the language and in everyday use as a word describing gossip. Eventually I came across Sea Pie, with it's many variations, and realised this was probably Scuttlebutt Pie. Originally a huge pie designed to keep the contents secure on a ship, and serve many hungry sailors. ●

# Northumberland duck

After weeks searching for this recipe, I was a little disappointed to find it is all about the presentation of a shoulder of lamb. However, shoulder of lamb is the cheapest, and some think the sweetest cut of lamb. You may need the assistance of a helpful butcher, and once again I called Chris at Harty Meats on the Isle of Sheppey to find and fillet my lamb joint. I think if it is done well, and you tell your guests to expect duck, they will be pleasantly surprised and amused when you reveal your 'duck', and they taste the roast lamb!

Serves 4-6  1.5-2 kg (3lb 5oz-4lb 6oz) shoulder of lamb

**2 cloves of garlic, sliced 250g (9oz) dried apricots Salt and pepper Olive oil Medium sherry, large wine glass Mint, bunch, finely chopped Rosemary, sufficient to place under lamb**

**NB** Ask your butcher to supply a shoulder with as much leg bone attached as possible. This is important. Also ask him to tunnel bone or fillet the shoulder. This means the blade-shaped bone is removed so that the shoulder stays whole. Keep the shoulder bone for later.

**METHOD**
Soak the apricots in the sherry for about 10 minutes. Drain them and mix well with the chopped mint. Reserve the sherry for use later in the gravy. Season with pepper and salt. Stuff the cavity left by the shoulder bone with the apricots and mint. Now you need to make the 'duck'. Take the leg, and twist up the section from the elbow to make the neck. Then take the last knuckle joint and bend 90° in the opposite direction to form the head. Hopefully, you have enough bone to split into a beak. Truss with string, to form a duck shape. Make a small cut in the rear end, and insert the blade bone, so that it resembles a tail! Now, make small incisions in the body of the lamb and push in slivers of sliced garlic. Rub all over with olive oil, salt and pepper. Sear and brown as best you can on top of your stove (might be difficult because of the shape). Lay the joint on a trivet in a roasting pan, and lay on a sprig or two of rosemary. Cover the duck's neck and head with tin foil, loosely.

Put in a pre heated oven at 180°C (350°F, gas 4), cook for 20 minutes per 450g (1lb) plus an extra 20 minutes. About 20 minutes before the end remove the tin foil from the head and neck. Test with a skewer to see if the juices are cooked to your liking. I think lamb should be slightly pink. When it is done to your liking, remove from the oven, transfer to a warm plate and cover with a clean tea towel. To make the gravy, skim off any excess fat from the juices in the roasting tin, then place the tin onto a hot hob and tip in the reserved sherry. Add a little water, or maybe some water from any vegetables you are cooking. Deglaze the pan by scraping as the liquid bubbles away. Have ready 25g (1oz) of butter mashed with a little cornflour, then add this slowly, whisking it bit by bit, to thicken your gravy. When you think it is ready, pour into a serving jug. Serve your 'duck' on a nest of rosemary. I would serve with lightly steamed cabbage cut into quarter wedges, and roughly crushed potatoes seasoned with butter and pepper. The gravy should be drizzled onto the potato.

# Toad in the hole

You all know this one! But maybe your children haven't been introduced to this very British dish of sausages in batter. The name refers to the appearance of the meat poking out of holes in the batter like toads peering out of their holes. It is actually a very old dish; the Romans hid all sorts of ingredients in their batter. More recently, pigeons would have been used instead of sausages, but it could be made with almost any chunks of often leftover meat. It is usually described as an economical dish, in other words, something for the hard up!

Mrs Beeton gives a recipe using steak and kidney, and describes the dish as homely but savoury. Nowadays, sausages are the norm for the meat, but you could substitute lamb chops for a more upmarket version.

Serves 4

**450g (1lb) good pork sausages**
**2 tbsp beef dripping**

To make the batter:
**225g (8oz) plain flour**
**3 eggs,**
**1/2 tsp salt**
**1/2 tsp mustard powder**
**600ml (20fl oz) milk**

## METHOD

First make the Yorkshire pudding batter. Into a mixing bowl, sift together the flour, salt and mustard powder. Make a well in the centre, and then break the eggs into the well. Then add a little milk and begin to stir and, still stirring, add the rest of the milk until you have a smooth creamy mixture. Cover with a tea towel and leave to stand for at least 30 minutes.

The important thing to remember about making any Yorkshire pudding recipe is that the fat in your oven tin must be really hot and smoking. But first, fry your sausages for about five minutes in the dripping, then pour the hot dripping into a preheated roasting dish.

Pour a little of the batter into the roasting dish and bake in a hot oven at 220°C (425°F, gas 7) until the batter sets, about another five minutes. Place your sausages in the pan, and pour in the remaining batter. Bake at the same high heat for about 30 minutes, until the pudding has risen. Serve with lightly steamed shredded cabbage, onion gravy, and maybe some pickle.

# Little pigs in blankets

"Scotland and the North of England are a rich source for odd-sounding recipes"

Here's an unusual recipe, probably more useful as a starter than as a main course. 'Pigs in blankets' means different things in different countries. In the States it is slang used by waiters in cafes – 'get me a Pig in blankets on wheels' translates as a takeaway ham sandwich. Americans would call this recipe by its other name, Angels on horseback. But I rather like the idea that the filling resembles little piglets. It reminds me of The Three Little Pigs children's story.

Serves 4

**3 or 4 oysters per person**
**Bacon, thinly sliced**
**Parsley**
**Toast**
**Pepper and salt**

**METHOD**

First shuck your oysters (remove from their shells), then season them with salt and pepper. Remove any fat from the bacon, and stretch each strip of bacon using the back of a knife. Wrap a strip of bacon around each oyster, like a blanket. Secure with a cocktail stick.

Heat a frying pan until it is really hot, and pop in the little pigs, taking care they don't burn by keeping them moving. It should only take about two minutes.

Remove and serve on small pieces of toast, garnished with parsley, and on a bed of watercress.

# Spotted Dick

Another classic British recipe, which has been neglected for too long. Now it is coming back into fashion and sophisticated restaurants are featuring it on their menus.

Spotted Dick is basically a rolypoly pudding. 'Dick' is old 19th Century slang for pudding, and the spots come from the raisins and currants. Suet puddings were around in the Middle Ages, but it wasn't until the 19th Century that they came into their own, with savoury as well as sweet versions. There is a variation called 'Spotted dog' – the difference is in the method, Spotted Dick is rolled up from a flat sheet, and Spotted dog is made from a solid cylinder of pudding. Both should be boiled in a pudding cloth, which is a skill sadly lacking these days, and so today we usually bake the pudding. I like to serve it with custard, of course, for that authentic old-fashioned taste.

Serves 4

**450g (1lb) self raising flour**
**225g (8oz) shredded suet**
**350g (12oz) raisins**
**Pinch of salt**
**50g (2oz) brown sugar**
**Zest of 1 orange**
**Millk**

For the custard:
**250ml (9fl oz) milk**
**150ml (¼ pint) cream**
**2 egg yolks**
**25g (1oz) caster sugar**
**Dash of orange juice**

## METHOD

Sift together the flour and salt, and add the shredded suet. Moisten with a little milk to make a stiff dough. Roll the dough out onto a floured board, so as to make a rectangle no wider than the saucepan you will use to cook the finished pudding. Roll it out until it is about 6mm (¼in) thick. Scatter the raisins evenly across the dough, then add the orange zest and sugar.

Carefully roll up into a sausage shape, and pinch the ends together. Take some muslin and cover with flour, then wrap around your pudding, securing the ends.

Put the pudding into a saucepan of boiling water. It is a good idea to have an up-turned plate in the bottom of the saucepan so that the pudding doesn't burn. Boil for about two hours, maybe two-and-a-half. While it is cooking, make the custard. Warm the milk and cream in a saucepan, and slowly bring to the boil. Then whisk together the egg yolks and sugar together until pale and fluffy. As soon as the milk boils, remove from the heat and whisk in the egg and sugar. Return to the heat, or place in a basin over simmering water, stirring continuously until thickened. The latter method is less likely to scramble the egg mixture. Homemade custard is much thinner than the packet version, and much nicer! I like my Spotted Dick with custard, but traditionally it was served with sifted sugar, cold butter, and lemon wedges.

# An eel odyssey

As **Clarissa Porter** explains eating eels has a "reputation" but don't worry she has plenty of traditional and tasty recipes

## Smoked eel salad with dill mustard mayonnaise

If you've never tried this before, get ready for a revelation. Of course, your main problem is going to be finding smoked eels. Some fishmongers sell imported smoked eel from Scandinavia, or you may be lucky to live near to a smokery. My local fishmonger doesn't stock the imported eels any more, he says they are too expensive for his customers. This would make an elegant starter, or a light supper.

Serves 4-6

smoked eel pieces, about 110g (3oz) to 175g (6oz) per person
baby salad leaves
a few walnuts
a few cubes of white bread doused in olive oil and fried to make croutons

For the mayonnaise
bunch of dill, finely chopped
1tbsp French mustard
2 egg yolks
250ml (8fl oz) of olive oil
2tbsp white wine vinegar

**METHOD**
First make the mayonnaise, with a whisk or in a blender, whisk the egg yolks and add the olive oil drip by drip until the sauce begins to thicken. Add the wine vinegar, then the mustard and finely chopped dill. If necessary, thin with a little cream. Then arrange a few eel slices on to the baby leaves, drizzle on the mayonnaise and scatter a few croutons, don't over do the croutons, the eels are such a subtle taste they shouldn't be smothered by another taste.

When I told my friends I would be cooking some traditional eel recipes, they all reacted with the same screwed-up noses and "yuk." Very few foods produce such a strong reaction, why is that I wonder? And though the eel is a true delicacy, I have even met fishmongers that have never tasted them. But, love them or loathe them they are part of our cooking heritage.

This extraordinary fish has been celebrated throughout recorded culinary history, from the Greeks and Romans, down to today. It has even given its name to places such as the Isle of Ely, and Eel Pie Island. Most people associate only one dish with eels, and that is of course jellied eels, and although my friends recoiled in distaste at the very idea of eating jellied eels, none had actually tried them. Which is a sorry state of affairs! So I am on a mission to promote The Appreciation of the Eel.

Firstly, an eel's life story. An extraordinary story that covers thousands of miles, and to this day is not completely documented. No one has yet succeeded in filming a complete lifecycle of an eel. Until quite recently people thought they came magically from the earth, or that they were a type of earthworm. Isaak Walton records in his book "The Compleat Angler," published in 1653, that some people believe they are formed from dew drops in the months of May and June, the Sun's heat turning the drops into eels!

The reality is just as strange. European eels spawn their young in the Sargasso Sea, near Bermuda. A female eel can produce 10 million larvae! The tiny transparent larvae drift on ocean currents for up to three years and over 3,000 miles till they reach our shores. When they arrive, they develop into tiny transparent 'Glass Eels'. When they enter freshwater, they become Elvers, and change colour and darken. As they grow, some travel upstream, and some migrate up and downstream. The further up river they go the more they change colour to brown or 'gold'. The females are more likely to migrate upstream, the males preferring to live in coastal areas. The females can live upstream for as long as 16 years. They can travel short distances over land, and burrow through sand for up to 30 miles! This explains how you can find eels in lakes and ponds far away from rivers. At some point in their lives, they feel the need to return to the sea, usually around September and October, when the sea is wild and stormy. They change colour again to a bluey silvery black, and begin the long swim back to the Sargasso Sea, where they spawn and die.

What an extraordinary story! Sadly, in the last 10 years, eel stocks have declined dramatically. This is nothing to do with over-fishing. It appears that a parasite is attacking the Eels, and stocks are perhaps 10 per cent of what they were in 1990. This means that there has been a dramatic increase in the price you'll be paying at the fishmongers. Eels are currently more expensive, kilo for kilo, than sea bass.

If you've never tasted eel, I can't recommend it enough. Eel has the firm texture of a prawn, and the light taste of plaice. Smoked eel is a true delicacy, but you'll have to search for it! I bought my eels at the Estuary Fish Merchants in Leigh on Sea in Essex. A real old-time enterprise situated in Cockle Shed Row. They have their own smokery and are happy to let you taste before you buy. Eels are sold live, so I recommend you ask the fishmonger to kill them for you! And clean and gut them, and remove the heads and skin. But please do try Eels, I guarantee you will be surprised and converted.

All the following recipes are traditional and very British. Eel pie and mash shops used to be a familiar sight around the country, particularly in London. Now they have all but disappeared, I know of two still operating, Goddards in Greenwich, and Manze in Peckham. Visiting these two establishments is an experience to be grabbed while you still can, they are remnants of a once thriving trade. •

# Eel pie

There are many variations to this essentially traditional dish. You can adapt it to your taste. A proper filling meal, straight out of the pages of Dickens or Shakespeare.

Serves 4-6

**750g (1½lb) – 1kg (2lb) eels, skinned, boned and sliced**
**25g (1oz) flour**
**2 slices of streaky bacon, chopped**
**1tbsp parsley, chopped**
**nutmeg**
**salt and pepper**
**3 hard boiled eggs, quartered**
**275ml (8fl oz) milk**
**225g (8oz) puff pastry (ready made)**
**1 egg, beaten**

## METHOD

Toss the eel pieces in flour seasoned with salt and pepper. Place the eel pieces in a greased baking tray and cover with greaseproof paper or foil and bake in an oven heated to 190ºC (375ºF, gas 5) for about 20 minutes. Remove from the oven. Grease a pie dish and place the eels and the bacon in the dish, then arrange the quartered hard-boiled eggs among the eel pieces. Season with pepper and salt and a few scrapes of nutmeg. Scatter parsley and pour over the milk. Roll out the puff pastry and cover the pie dish. Decorate the pastry with left over pieces and glaze with the egg yolk. Return to the oven and bake for 20 to 25 minutes until the pastry has risen and is golden brown. Serve with crushed potatoes (if you like you can add chopped spring onions to the mash), and mushy peas.

## "Eel has the firm texture of a prawn, and the light taste of plaice"

# Isaak Walton's roast eel

"The Compleat Angler" published in 1653 has a chapter devoted to eels. This is the recipe from that chapter, only slightly adapted for now. I suggest you try and stick as much to the original recipe as possible, and I promise you this is a really excellent dish. They certainly knew how to cook their fish 350 years ago! What an adventure it must have been to have travelled with Mr Walton. This is a truly simple magnificent dish, shut your eyes and be transported back 350 years to the banks of the Thames alongside Isaak Walton.

**1 eel (depending on the size, would serve 2 or 3 people)**
**110g (3½oz) butter**
**nutmeg**
**pepper**
**salt**
**'sweet herbs' such as marjoram, oregano, tarragon, parsley**
**Spinach leaves**
**2 anchovy fillets**

### ISAAK WALTON'S METHOD

Prepare your eel, remove the head. Wash the eel in water and salt. Then pull off the skin down to near the tail, but don't completely remove it. Now gut the eel, but don't wash it any more. Make 3 or 4 scotches (slices, cuts, slashes) in the side of the eel. Into those scotches and into the belly cavity put the sweet herbs, the anchovy and a little nutmeg cut very small and mixed with butter and salt. Then you pull the skin back over the eel and tie it where the head was. Tie it tight. Then Isaak would have tied the eel to a spit and roasted it over an open fire, basting with water and salt till the skin burst. Then after a final basting with butter, the eel would be served with the juices as its own sauce.

### CLARISSA PORTER'S METHOD

Remove the skin and guts from the eel, cut into pieces about 4 inches long. Place some spinach leaves on some foil and lay the eel pieces on top. Make a few slashes in the side of the eel. Mix together the nutmeg, herbs, butter, pepper, salt and anchovies chopped, and stuff inside the eel and into the cuts in the body. Place more spinach leaves on top of the fish, make a parcel of the foil and bake for about 30 minutes in a moderate oven, or for slightly less time on a barbecue. Serve with sliced boiled potatoes.

## "Eels are sold live, so ask the fishmonger to kill them for you"

# Jellied eels

You really must try jellied eels. They are deliciously light and cool with a subtle taste. Tradition, history, its all there on your plate!

Serves 4-6

**900g (2lb) eels, skinned and cut into pieces about 1 inch long**
**juice of one lemon**
**6 peppercorns**
**1 small onion, quartered**
**parsley**
**bay leaf**

### METHOD

Place the eels in a pan of warm water, add all the other ingredients except the parsley, bring to the boil and simmer for about 30 minutes. Then lift out the eel pieces. Skim off any froth from the liquid with a piece of stale bread. Strain the liquid, and then strain again. Place the pieces of eel in a serving bowl and pour in the now cool liquid. Stir in the chopped parsley. Serve, with brown bread and maybe salad leaves.

# Asparagus Tips!

This long, slim delicacy is in season now and **Clarissa Porter** is very, very excited

The first of May marks the start of the asparagus season and, if we're lucky, two months of sheer tastebud pleasure from this slim, sought-after vegetable. Yes, I know it is available in supermarkets all year round, but the home-grown seasonal product is uniquely superior to imported asparagus, and these days we have to think of the 'food miles'.

I noticed my local Tesco selling fresh asparagus from Peru – the world's leading exporter – but, as far as I'm concerned, you can't beat the English variety. It's the best in the world. And even better when bought from a nearby farm shop or, in my case, a roadside stall, selling asparagus fresh from a smallholding or back garden. Aim to buy direct from the grower and eat it as fresh as possible.  Asparagus is a member of the lily family, and so related to onions, leeks, garlic, and tulips. It is one of the earliest recorded vegetables and mentioned in the earliest of cook books, such as the 3rd Century volume De re Coquinaria by the Roman Apicius, and first mentioned in English writing in the 11th Century.

Asparagus is grown all over the world, wherever the climate is temperate and the soil suitable. England is about as far north as it is possible for successful asparagus cultivation. The Ancient Egyptians grew it, as did the Romans and the Greeks, who both left instructions for cultivation. Besides eating large quantities of asparagus, the Romans used it medicinally, for instance as a pain reliever when extracting teeth! In fact, the Romans had a special fleet of ships to fetch supplies from around their empire. In order to store it, they sent it by chariot to the snowy Alps to keep it fresh for the Feast of Epicurius. They even had a saying, attributed to the Emperor Augustus: "As quick as cooking asparagus", to describe speed.

Originally a wild plant, the name comes from the Greek asparagos, which means 'shoot' or 'sprout'. In this country it was originally known as sperage, which evolved into 'sparagus' and then into the charming 'Sparrow-Grass'. Later the Latin name 'Asparagus Officinalis' came into use, and we all began to call it asparagus.

## Posh plant

Down the centuries asparagus has been a sign of elegance and wealth, which is probably why there is so much history written about this wonderful plant. Samuel Pepys in his diary writes on four occasions of buying asparagus in 17th Century London. He mentions eating it as a midnight snack! In Pepys' time London was full of asparagus gardens. In those days it was tied into bundles of 20 spears, known as a 'round'. And six rounds were tied together to go to market. I believe this practice has died out, but you can still see a recreation of the old ways of selling asparagus every year at The Fleece Inn, in Bretforton, Worcestershire, during the Asparagus Festival.

As you might expect, there is a wealth of recipes using asparagus, but perhaps you will be surprised to know that asparagus is also grown and celebrated in America. Early settlers took plants on the hazardous voyage to the Americas, but wild asparagus was already growing in North, Central, and South America.

There are many early, interesting recipes from the 16th and 17th centuries, from the kitchens of the Great Houses of the plantations. The cotton plantations usually had extensive asparagus beds and Thomas Jefferson and Benjamin Franklin both mention the plant in their letters. However, when I was growing up it was conspicuously absent from my diet. I first encountered asparagus as soup, courtesy of Campbell's! Cream of Asparagus was considered the height of sophistication in my parent's house. My husband's first encounter was with a sweet tasting, squishy green, unidentifiable stick on fingers of brown bread at his first place of work. It was part of his job to clear-up at company seminars. After the speeches and the slide show, visitors were treated to canapés and drinks. He had the worst possible introduction – tinned, limp, and merging with stale bread. He wasn't sure what it was...

## Asparagus growers

Thankfully, we now look forward with enthusiasm to the beginning of May, when we take a trip to our favourite growers, Carolyn and Peter Andrews.

They grow and sell asparagus from their picture postcard cottage, near Teynham in Kent. Many years ago we were scouting for just such a cottage to use in a photograph, and after driving around for a nearly a day we happened upon this perfect little thatched dwelling down a narrow lane. Carolyn was only too happy to help us out by letting us use her cottage. While we were talking to her she told us about her asparagus, then took us into her garden to show off the rows of plants. She explained that, although it's a perennial, and therefore you don't have to replant every year, it is very labour intensive.

The asparagus grows in ridges and when it is ready to be harvested, the plants have to be cut every day. (Carolyn eschews using a special asparagus knife in favour of an ordinary Stanley knife fitted with a miniature hacksaw blade).

Then the spears have to be graded by thickness (there are five recognised grades of thickness), trimmed, washed, and weighed into bundled bunches. Despite all the work it is a high value crop, and in a good year it yields three tons per acre! Which is a lot of asparagus.

We returned when the season began and bought some of her delicious crop. Since then we've been going back year after year. Carolyn's output has grown for she has acquired a share of the field behind her cottage. On a recent visit, the asparagus had yet to appear, but I found her out in the field, mending fences. "It's a constant battle against the rabbits!" she said.

# Asparagus omelette with shrimps

A delicious light lunch, the freshest of asparagus and the fluffy, eggy omelette taste combine with the shrimps to make a healthy satisfying meal.

Serves 4

**1 bunch of steamed asparagus, maybe 12 medium spears, trimmed in half**
**8 large free range eggs, beaten**
**Salt and pepper**
**1 tsp parsley, finely chopped**
**100g (4oz) peeled brown shrimps**
**1 spring onion, finely chopped**
**1 tsp plain flour**
**75g (3oz) butter, cut into cubes**

**METHOD**

Whisk the eggs in a bowl, with the pepper, salt and the chopped parsley. Stir in the shrimps and spring onions. Sprinkle with the flour and 25g (1oz) of the chopped butter. Melt the remaining butter in a pan and, when the butter starts to brown, pour in the egg mixture.

Stir around the edges so that the liquid escapes from underneath. Add the asparagus (tips only) and cook for a few more seconds. Slide the omelette onto a hot serving plate and pour over the butter from the pan.

Serve with a simple green salad.

If you're travelling along the A2 between Sittingbourne and Faversham, you'll see her sign, 'Fresh Cut Asparagus', at the roadside, directing you to her cottage. I recommend a visit. Or you can contact her by e-mail at: carpenter@dialstart.net

## Choosing and using

Fresh asparagus should have firm, dark green shoots with maybe a hint of purple at the tip. The spears should be straight, and the tip should be closed. Once picked, asparagus can be stored for at the most three weeks, just above freezing, and in fairly (80 per cent) high humidity.

Preferably, you should eat your asparagus as soon after picking as possible. It provides a very good source of Vitamin A and Folic acid. The latter is very important in the production of blood cells, and for a healthy liver. Pregnant women need a good supply of Folic Acid, so they should eat lots of asparagus. It is also rich in calcium and potassium and is low in fat, cholesterol and sodium, and almost calorie neutral. Pretty much the ideal food!

I think the best way of cooking asparagus is to steam it. You can buy specialist steamers but it isn't necessary as long as you have a suitably deep steamer. Take your bunch of asparagus, tie it together with string and stand it upright in the steamer, and steam for about 20 minutes.

Or you can take your tied bunch and stand it upright in a deep saucepan so that the water comes about halfway up the stems. The water should be boiling – cook for about 20-25 minutes, testing for tenderness by piercing the bottom of the stalk with the point of a knife.

The bottoms of the asparagus, which are tougher, boil and the tips steam. The best of both methods... But whatever, don't overcook. Even early cookbooks emphasised the importance of not overcooking green vegetables.

You may have seen or eaten white asparagus, either imported fresh or in tins or jars. White asparagus is produced by growing the plants in the dark, so they have no chlorophyl. This is usually done by simply making the ridges taller and cutting the asparagus before it is exposed to daylight. I'm a bit of a food purist, and I think the only asparagus worth eating is the green variety!

The plants grown in this country grow slowly and therefore have the most intense flavour. Much better than those grown in Spain, for instance, where a shorter growing time means the plants shoot up and have less flavour. Similarly, I think it is best to eat asparagus during that two-month seasonal period when they are naturally ready. But you may disagree and, after all, Louis 14th of France, who was a fan of all things vegetable, built greenhouses so that he could force asparagus for harvesting all year-round. If you want to grow your own, all you need is suitably sandy, loamy soil, well drained. You can grow from nodules (seeds) or crowns (plants), but once planted you will have to wait (patiently) one, two or even three seasons, depending on whether you've started with seeds or plants. Then you will have asparagus for years to come. The old English variety, 'Connivers Colossal', would last for 25 seasons, but the newer Dutch varieties may only last for 10. Still worthwhile, I think you'll agree. Asparagus is a perennial, so although it is labour intensive during the season, you only have to plant once in 20 years! ●

# Rustic asparagus

So you've been for a drive in the country, and found the perfect little stall selling fresh asparagus. Back home, here's the best way to eat it – outdoors, accompanied by friends and a bottle of chilled wine. This one's a bit of a DIY dish and great fun for get-togethers.

Serves 4-6

**2 bunches of asparagus**
**1 hard-boiled egg per person**
**25g (1oz) melted butter per person**
**Pepper mill**

**METHOD**
Steam the Asparagus for about 20 minutes, depending on the thickness. Test for tenderness by piercing with the point of a sharp knife. Put the hard-boiled eggs in a bowl, and the melted butter in a small jug. Have a pepper mill handy.

Offer the eggs and tell your companions to shell them and remove the yolks, discarding the whites. Each person can mash their egg with a little butter and season with pepper, and then dip their Asparagus into the resulting mixture.

Fingers rather than forks!

# Sparrow-grass bread

This is a very old recipe. There is a version in *The Art of Cookery*, written by Hannah Glass and published in London in 1747. Once again it is a familiar recipe in America. I think this is because in the 18th Century America was still a colony and we shared a common culinary heritage. It is known that George Washington and Thomas Jefferson both owned a copy of the book.

Hannah Glass believed that asparagus shouldn't be over cooked: "over-boiling took away the sweetness and the beauty," she said.

Serves 4

**1 small French roll per person**
**20 fresh, thin asparagus spears**
**4 tsp butter 6 egg yolks, beaten**
**500ml (18fl oz) single cream**
**½ tsp ground nutmeg**
**Salt**

### METHOD

Take the French rolls and slice off the top crusts; put to one side but keep each crust with its matching bottom half. Scoop out the crumbs from the bottom halves of the rolls. In the top crusts, make a few holes with the end of a wooden spoon, two or three per roll. Melt the butter in a pan, and brown the rolls on all sides.

Rinse the asparagus, cutting off any woody parts. Place in a steamer and steam for about 20 minutes, no longer. Drain. Cut the tips of 12 spears so they are about 75mm (3in) long, and put to one side. Take the remaining section of asparagus and the rest of the cooked asparagus and cut them into 25mm (1in) lengths.

In another pan, warm the cream and nutmeg, and stir in the beaten egg yolks. Season with salt and keep stirring on a gentle heat to make a thick sauce. Add the 25mm lengths to the sauce and stir well, gradually bringing to the boil. Be careful not to end up with scrambled egg! Remove from the heat. Fill the rolls with the mixture, then with the reserved asparagus tips, placing them in the holes you made in the top crusts so that the asparagus looks as if it is growing from the roll. Serve straight away, hot.

# Asparagus with Dublin Bay prawns in a saffron broth

A simple elegant, summery lunch. You can simply enjoy this soupy stew and follow it with a large bowl of fresh strawberries.

Serves 4

**4 large Dublin Bay prawns, uncooked**
**300ml (½ pint) fish stock (from a cube will do)**
**Pinch of saffron strands**
**½ glass of dry white wine**
**½ turnip**
**1 carrot**
**1 courgette**
**8 asparagus tips, fairly large asparagus**
**Salt and pepper**
**Bunch of fresh basil**

### METHOD

Prepare the vegetables by either cutting into strips or into four ovals, the size of quails eggs. Warm the stock and infuse the saffron into it. Lightly poach the prawns in the stock until they turn pink. Remove them and put to one side. Now poach all the vegetables except the asparagus tips, then remove them and reserve to one side. Add the wine to the stock and bubble away for a minute or two.

Add the asparagus tips and cook these until tender, not very long. Then add the vegetables and prawns that you have put to one side. Warm everything through and then serve in shallow dishes scattered with torn basil.

# Wild about samphire

***Clarissa Porter***
takes us in search of
samphire – a cross
between spinach and
seaweed

**M**ay is a little early for samphire, but I thought if you didn't know about this intriguing coastal plant, you may need a little notice because I hope to persuade you to get out on the marshes and pick your own! For Free!

June would be the earliest to find wild samphire in its juiciest condition. There are several species, but I am only concerned here with Marsh Samphire and Rock Samphire. As their names suggest, you'll find them either on marshland, or on shingle beaches and cliffs, and I think Marsh Samphire is superior in taste.

These are not plants you'll find in your local supermarket, even during their season, although you may find Marsh Samphire in your fishmonger's display, and on the menu of trendy restaurants and pubs in season. But it is all but impossible to buy out of season.

## In search of samphire

Around the country there are samphire gatherers, who search the marshes and scramble around cliffs, foraging for samphire to sell, either at the roadside, or to restaurants and fishmongers. Small outfits have sprung up to try and organise these elusive individuals into something more orderly and profitable. One such is Forager, based in Canterbury and founded by two dedicated hunters of free wild country food (www.forager.org.uk).

I tried to find a real samphire gatherer to talk to but, rather like the plant they hunt, they proved elusive. So I resolved to get out there in my wellies, at low tide, and try to find my own samphire. Just in case I didn't, a little research turned up a company called Salty Greens, that promised they could send me fresh samphire by mail order, and sea lavender if I wanted. I found them helpful and enthusiastic – you can contact them at www.saltygreens.com

Then I discovered that a company called The Fish Society supplied frozen samphire, although they did, very honestly, say that it didn't freeze very well and when defrosted turned to mush (www.thefishsociety.co.uk). However, the late great Jane Grigson says in her book, English Food, that samphire freezes very well, if first blanched. The nice man at The Fish Society admitted they hadn't blanched so far but they might, now, be doing so in future.

I'm not advocating buying out of season like this, but I do appreciate that trekking across muddy salt marshes is not everyone's cup of tea. As for rock climbing for Rock Samphire, well, there is a famous print called The Samphire Gatherer, which shows a hapless woman clinging to a cliff face, wielding a sort of shepherd's crook to collect her precious, elusive samphire.

And there is an equally famous quote from King Lear: "Half-way down hangs one that gathers samphire; dreadful trade". Shakespeare's samphire gatherer was one of the cliff-climbing variety. It seems that samphire gatherers were to be pitied for their dangerous and probably dirty job. But all the hardships are worth it, because samphire is unique, somewhere between seaweed and spinach. In fact it is part of the same family as spinach, and beetroot. A special taste which goes well with fish, obviously, and lamb.

## Also known as...

Samphire gets its name from 'St Peter's Herb'. In French it is sampier, from Saint Pierre. In Italy it

# Romney Marsh lamb chops with samphire

This recipe is a natural marriage of the famous Romney Marsh lamb and the samphire that is found where the marsh meets the sea.

Serves 4

For the lamb:
**2 lamb chops per person**
**Juice and zest of 1 orange**
**2 cloves of garlic, crushed**
**Freshly milled sea salt, and pepper**

For the samphire:
**1 quantity of samphire per person, about a handful**
**100g (4oz) melted, unsalted butter**
**Juice of 1/2 an orange**
**1 tbsp chopped capers**
**Pepper**

## METHOD

To prepare your fresh samphire, pick over and remove any really woody bits. Cut into pieces about 10cm (4in) long at the most. Wash then rinse to remove any sand or grit.

Now place the chops in a shallow dish and drizzle over the juice from the orange and a little of the zest. Smear the crushed garlic across each chop. Season with pepper and salt. Cover and leave in the fridge for at least 20 minutes. Then, grill the chops for three or four minutes each side, using a little olive oil. They should remain pink inside.

Meanwhile, place the samphire in a steamer and steam for about 15 minutes until tender. If you have a lot of samphire, and can afford to just use the tastiest tips, the cooking time will be shorter. Mix with a few chopped capers, orange juice, and melted butter.

Serve the chops on a bed of Samphire, simply. Drizzle the meat juices over the chops, and serve with a side dish of plain boiled new potatoes.

# Roast monkfish with samphire and garlic

Samphire is the perfect companion to all things fishy, and monkfish is a sweet, firm counterpoint to the delicate crispiness of the wild samphire.

Serves 4-6

**1.4kg (3lb 1oz) monkfish tail, marinated**
**Quantity of washed, prepared samphire (about a handful per person)**
**4 spring onions, sliced lengthways**
**1 sprig of baby vine tomatoes, left on the vine (6-8 tomatoes)**

For the marinade:
**2 crushed cloves of garlic**
**1 spring onion, finely chopped**
**Small glass of dry white wine**
**1/2 a wine glass of olive oil**
**Pepper & salt.**

## METHOD

Mix the marinade and put the fish with the marinade in a plastic bag in your fridge for one or two hours. Turn the bag from time to time to distribute the marinade. Preheat the oven to 190°C (375°F, gas 5).

Place the clean samphire in a large oven dish and place the fish on top. Lay the spring onions on the fish and the tomatoes alongside. Pour the marinade over the dish, and cook for 25-30 minutes, basting occasionally with the juices.

Serve simply from the oven dish.

is dedicated to fishermen, because St Peter is the patron saint of fishermen. It is also known as 'Sea Fennel' and 'Glasswort', because it was used in the manufacture of glass. Samphire has a high sodium carbonate content, and when it was burned the resulting salt was mixed with sand to manufacture glass. It was also used for the manufacture of soap. It is rich in oil and protein, and in other parts of the world is used for animal feed. But don't let that put you off! Samphire is thought of highly enough for it to have been served at the wedding breakfast of Prince Charles and Lady Diana.

Most of you probably only discovered this vegetable in the last 10 years, as it has become championed by celebrity chefs on the look out for ever more obscure traditional and real ingredients.

But it has been around and in everyday use for a long time. In the middle ages it was sold on the streets of London, with the cries 'Crest Marine' and, later, 'Camphire'. It was used in salads, and pickled, and used as a medicine, of course. It was thought to cure all sorts of intestinal disorders.

A word of caution before you venture out onto the marshes, be mindful of tides and mud. Samphire grows on the edges, where the sea washes over and retreats. You are looking for a small, bright green succulent plant, with a strong scent and slightly woody in appearance – like a tiny Monkey Puzzle tree.

It is found all around our coast, but most plentifully in Wales, East Anglia, Kent and Lincolnshire. Rock Samphire is found on shingle beaches, at the foot of cliffs, and on the cliffs themselves. Shakespeare's gatherer plied his trade on the cliffs at Dover. At nearby Ramsgate an area has been renamed Samphire Hoe. I have seen Rock Samphire growing plentifully at the edge of the Swale in Kent. Rock Samphire is also a succulent, but with small leaves.

Both samphires have a typically salty taste. They can be eaten raw, or steamed, boiled, fried, pickled, or as a flavouring in mustard. When you collect your samphire, cut it above the ground – it is illegal to pull it up by the roots – and only take what you can use for yourself and your family. Here are a few traditional recipes for this wild and aromatic plant. ●

# Scallops with samphire and bacon

Known in France as Coquilles St Jacques, after a legend involving St James and rescue from the sea, scallops are sweet and tender and go well with samphire. I used King Scallops, the best I think, and the finest come from Scotland, where divers gather them from the sea bed. You can buy them live in the shell, or pre-cooked. If you buy live, open the shell with a long-bladed knife, discard the eyes and the 'beard', and rinse, not soak, them under a tap. Cook them as quickly as possible.

Serves 4

**12 King Scallops, removed from their shells and cleaned**
**1 small carton of single cream**
**Knob of butter**
**4 slices of back bacon, cut into strips**
**4 handfuls of washed, uncooked samphire**
**Pepper**

## METHOD
Pour the carton of cream, together with the butter, into a shallow frying pan. Warm the cream. Add the scallops, place a lid on the pan, and gently poach for about three minutes. Remove the scallops from the pan, keep warm, and reserve the juice from the pan in a jug. Wipe the pan, and fry the bacon strips until the fat begins to melt. Add the samphire to the bacon, and cook for a few minutes, shaking the pan. Season with pepper.

Serve the scallops on top of the samphire, and drizzle with some of the reserved juice. Serve with brown bread and butter.

"I tried to find a real samphire gatherer to talk to but, rather like the plant they hunt, they proved elusive."

# Sarah Bernhardt's larks with samphire

This unusual and exotic dish is one of several recipes associated with the famous actress, Sarah Bernhardt. I don't know whether it was created in her honour, or if it is a dish she prepared. The original recipe calls for larks, for which I've substituted small poussins, but you could try any small bird – pigeon, quail, or guinea fowl, perhaps. This recipe is from an age when surprise and innovation were prized as much as culinary skills. Thankfully, it's also very tasty, and serves as a reminder of how samphire was once considered a celebrity dish.

Serves 1-2

Apart from the birds, the amounts are discretionary!

**3 small poussins**
**Butter**
**Samphire, washed**
**Raisins**
**Breadcrumbs**
**Milk**
**Juniper berries, crushed**
**Fatty bacon**
**Olive oil**
**METHOD**
Soak some breadcrumbs in a little milk. Remove the flesh from two of the poussins and discard the carcasses. Put the meat into a mortar together with a little butter. Pound together, then add the drained breadcrumbs, a few raisins, and a few crushed juniper berries. Chop a little samphire and add to the mixture, and pound again, so that everything is well mixed into a coarse paste.

Take the third poussin, and stuff the mixture into the bird. Rub olive oil all over the poussin and cover with samphire and a strip of fatty bacon. Roast on a spit, if possible, or in an oven at 180°C (350°F, gas 4) for 30-45 minutes, until the juices run clear when you pierce the bird with a skewer.

Just before serving, make a crouton big enough for the poussin to sit on. Soak the crouton in gin, then toast it and butter it. Serve the poussin on the crouton, with a little samphire as an accompaniment.

Wow! Encore!

# Come to the fete

## Enjoy all the fun of the fayre with some recipes that go down a treat, by *Clarissa Porter*

# Orange and lemon cakes

I usually make vast quantities (10) of these cakes for the local fete. They sell them whole, but they could be sliced and sold in smaller portions. They look so pretty wrapped in baking paper tied with string or red ribbon, and with a little sprig of rosemary or marigold tied into the bow.

I bake them in small loaf tins that are greased and then have a strip of grease proof paper inside to hoist the finished cake from the tin.

For one cake:
**2 eggs**
**100g (4oz) butter**
**100g (4oz) self-raising flour**
**100g (4oz) sugar**
**Zest of 1 lemon, or half and half, lemon and orange**

For the topping:
**Juice of one orange or lemon, or mixed orange and lemon**
**1 tbsp granulated sugar**

### METHOD

Weigh the eggs and that is the weight of butter, flour and sugar you should use – usually about 100g.

In a blender, cream together the butter, flour, sugar and eggs. Stir in the zest. Pile the mixture into a small greased loaf tin and bake in an oven pre-heated to about 180°C (350°F, gas 4) for 25 minutes or until a skewer inserted comes out clean. Remove from the oven.

Combine the granulated sugar and the juice, and pour over the cake, then put back in the oven for a few more minutes. Remove and cool. Decorate with a curl or two of zest.

At the time of year when the fete season is looming, my neighbour Penny comes knocking on my door, hoping to enlist my help cooking cakes for the local fete – the Hillyfields Fayre. We live in a conservation area and the local Brockley Society has been holding this annual fete for more than 30 years. It began in a very small way, with a small group of public-spirited locals cobbling together a handful of stalls, determined to enjoy themselves whatever the weather. Like topsy it has grown and grown. For the society, it is the major fundraising event of the year.

Dozens of stalls sell homemade produce and plants, and of course bric-a-brac. It's traditional fun with a coconut shy, tug o'war, and donkey rides. The fire brigade let youngsters play with their fire engine, the sound of the siren mixing with the music of the local steel bands. And then there's the fabled barbeque.

The biggest tent houses the cake stall, organised by Penny and manned by her two daughters. Their stall is usually the most successful. Previously they raised over £400 just from cakes and teas. The most popular cakes are the 'naughtiest' ones – chocolate or strawberry cakes always sell out first! I've been contributing cakes for more years than I care to remember, and also always enter the flower display competition, just using whatever is available from my garden, with props like old boots and string.

All around the country, the fete season is in full swing, ranging from quite large events like the Hillyfields Fayre to smaller, more intimate country church fetes where everyone seems to know everyone, and the vicar strolls around beaming, weather permitting! Fetes as we know them seem to have originated in Victorian times and probably grew from the annual picnics or garden parties large landowners would hold for their workers and their families. Soon they were adopted as annual events by the local parish churches.

Before this they were highly ceremonial affairs, rather like the Queen's garden parties today. Sober and probably a bit stodgy. In 1811 the Prince Regent held a fete in honour of the recently exiled French Royal Family, and invited 2000 guests. So it wasn't really a fete, but George III was so ill that the rowdy celebratory Regency romp was called a 'fete' for reasons of decorum!

Wherever they are held – at schools, churches or community centres – they are a very good way for the local community to come together and get to know each other, meet new friends and build a sense of belonging. Did you know that John Lennon was introduced to Paul McCartney for the first time at Woolton Parish Fete in 1957? See where a chance meeting at a church fete might take you!

# Disappearing strawberry cream tarts

This isn't Alice in Wonderland, they are simply so delicious that they vanish!

**For the pastry:**
**150g (5oz) plain flour**
**Pinch of salt**
**75g (3oz) butter**
**1 tsp sugar**
**1 egg yolk, beaten**
**2 tbsp of very cold water**

**For the filling:**
**450g (1lb) strawberries**
**100g (4oz) cream cheese**
**Icing sugar, a little to taste**
**3 tbsp double cream**
**Dash of almond or vanilla essence**
**4 tbsp strawberry jam, melted**

### METHOD
Heat your oven to 190°C (375°F, gas 5). Grease a dozen small cake moulds. Sift together the flour, salt and sugar into a bowl. Cut the butter into small pieces and rub in to the flour with your fingertips until it looks like bread crumbs. Mix in the beaten egg and water, quickly, using a knife. The mixture will come together as a dough. Turn onto a floured board and knead gently. Wrap in cling film and put into your fridge for 30 minutes.

Then, remove from the fridge and roll out onto a floured board. Cut 12 little circles to fit your moulds.

Bake blind for eight minutes, remove and allow to cool.

Now, wash and hull the strawberries. If they are very large you may need to slice them. Warm the strawberry jam and brush a little inside each pastry case. Mix the cheese, cream, essence and sugar together. Fill each pastry case with a little of the cream mixture and arrange a few strawberries on top.

Carefully brush the rest of the melted strawberry jam over the top. Place on a pretty plate.

Close your eyes. When you open them, the tarts will be gone!

My absolute favourite church fete is held every year in Kent at St Thomas' on the old Isle of Harty. Actually, it's no longer an island but part of the Isle of Sheppey. But as you approach on the bumpy single-track lane across the marshes, the Church rising up ahead of you, it is easy to imagine Harty as an island still.

St Thomas' is probably the most remote church in Kent. Attending a service there is a magical experience, like being transported back in time. The 900-year-old church is so remote that it has no electricity – candles and oil lamps light the church. Perhaps because of this it recently featured in a film of Dickens' Great Expectations.

For the last 28 years locals have held their annual Flower Festival in the beautiful churchyard overlooking the Swale. "The festival is the only way we have of raising money for the upkeep of the church," says Churchwarden Colin Patience, "the church is so remote that we only have a service once a month, and we can't have the usual coffee mornings or whist drives that might provide some income."

The Festival is always held on the first weekend of July. The tiny church is filled with flowers donated by the local people and, as you walk in, you're struck by the fragrance of sweet peas and the beautiful light cast by the stained glass windows falling upon the tiny pieces of mismatched carpet brought by the congregation to use as hassocks.

The churchyard is filled with stalls run by local people, selling jams and cakes, honey and flowers. There are demonstrations of craft, such as corn dolly making, and there will be country dancing. On the Sunday the Salvation Army band will play. One of the regular stallholders is Barbara Newberry, who makes jams to sell at the church. At the festival you'll find her selling hanging baskets and flowers. Her jams are on sale inside the church all year round, just remember to use the honesty box.

Churchwarden Colin has a stall selling corn dollies and he shows people how to make their own. His corn dollies are on sale in the nearby Harty Ferry Inn, all proceeds going to St Thomas'.

If you live anywhere near this part of Kent I urge you to visit the festival. Poet Laureate John Betjeman, apologising for missing the festival, once wrote:

"Alas I shall have to console myself with memories of the Church in its splendid isolation, with sea birds wheeling by and the Thames so wide as to be open sea, and air so fresh as to be healthier than yoghourt (unflavoured)."

Thankfully the church is open all year round, so if you can't make the festival you can still experience this unique place at any time of the year. It is especially evocative during the bleak winter months.

Recipes for fetes should be simple and pleasing, here are some ideas for your local fete. •

# Granny cakes

My mother-in-law used to make dozens of these when we were students. When our daughter was born they became her favourite cakes and she christened them 'Granny cakes'.

They seem very popular at our local fete as well, disappearing as fast as we replenish the stocks. Best eaten fresh and warm, when they crumble in the hand and melt in the mouth.

**100g (4oz) butter, softened
2 eggs, beaten
175g (6oz) self-raising flour
2 handfuls of mixed dried fruit
Vanilla essence**

**METHOD**
Take a big old-fashioned mixing bowl and a wooden spoon (mother-in-laws always used a wooden spoon!), beat the softened butter and the sugar until smooth and creamy. Add the beaten eggs and vanilla essence (a drop or two), and beat some more. Sift in the flour using an old-fashioned sieve, from a great height. This introduces air to the mixture. Fold in the flour using that wooden spoon, and then the dried fruit.

Fill as many little paper cake cases as you can, and line them up on a baking sheet. Place in an oven pre-heated to 180°C (350°F, gas 4) for about 25 minutes, or until golden and risen. You will smell them when they are cooked.

Cool and dust with sugar. If they are not eaten straight away they keep very well in a cake tin for midnight feasts!

# Sweet and savoury scones

A favourite at garden parties and fetes, beloved of vicars up and down the land!

For the sweet variety:
**225g (8oz) self-raising flour**
**Pinch of salt**
**50g (2oz) butter**
**50g (2oz) sugar**
**150ml (¼ pint) milk**
**50g (2oz) dried fruit**
**½ tsp bicarbonate of soda**
**1 egg, beaten for the glaze**
**Salt**

For the savoury variety use the same ingredients as for the sweet, but omit the fruit and sugar, and replace with:

**50g (2oz) mixed olives, pitted and chopped**
**2 tbsp chopped fresh herbs – parsley, basil or thyme.**

For the pesto butter:
**50g (2oz) basil and coriander leaves**
**2 cloves garlic**
**2 tbsp pine nuts**
**50g (2oz) Parmesan, grated**
**75g (3oz) butter**
**Pepper and salt**

**METHOD** (sweet scones)
Rub the butter into the flour with your fingers, adding the bicarbonate of soda and the sugar, and season with a pinch of salt. Then add the milk, folding in with a knife to make a dough.

Then fold in the dried fruit. Roll out on a floured board to a thickness of about 12mm (½in), and then cut into 40mm (1½in) rounds.

Place on greased baking sheet, glaze with a little beaten egg on the tops and bake for 12-15 minutes in an oven heated to 190°C (375°F, gas 5).

Serve with lashings of strawberry jam and whipped cream.

**METHOD** (savoury scones)
Follow the above method, but leave out the sugar and fruit and replace with the olives and herbs.

For the pesto butter, just put all the ingredients in a food processor and whizz for a few seconds. Store in your fridge until needed. Serve with a smear of the pesto butter.

# Life is just a bowl of cherries!

***Clarissa Porter*** helps you live for the day and make the most of cherries – their season is all too short

**J**une marks the beginning of the cherry season in England, and the red varieties 'Early River' and 'Kentish Reds' should soon be ready to pick. The cherry orchards of Kent will be bursting with heavily laden fruit trees as the long-anticipated summer becomes reality.

I always associate cherries with my childhood, holding a handful in one hand, then picking them from the stalks with my teeth, and hanging pairs of cherries over my ears to mimic the adults' earrings. Then, later, in my teens, when horse riding took over my life, riding through cherry orchards near my home in Barming, picking cherries from the trees as I went – surely one of the happiest carefree memories anyone can have. Those old cherry orchards have all but disappeared now, but there is a traditional orchard that I know of, where sheep still graze among the cherry trees, which stand more than 40 feet high.

It is at Allens Farm, near Sevenoaks. The Webb family raise sheep and grow fruit on their determinedly traditional and organic farm. Their cherry orchard is more than 100 years old. If you would like to vsit and buy their meat or fruit (they also grow damsons and cobnuts) contact them at info@allensfarm.co.uk.

The English cherry season is so fleeting, even though supermarkets seem to stock them nearly all year round. Traditionally the season was heralded by cherry fairs, which were held all over the country, and all over Europe and America.

You can still find a cherry fair in Chertsey, Surrey. It is known as the Black Cherry Fair, and was founded in 1440 by Royal Charter. Chertsey had four fairs – the onion fair, the horse fair, the goose fair, and the black cherry fair. The latter is traditionally held on the second Saturday in July, on Abbey Field. Contact admin@blackcherryfair.com for more information.

## Cherry cultivation

Cultivation originated in Asia minor, then gradually spread across the Old World, the Romans being instrumental in the spread of this delicious fruit. It was, of course, wild and cultivating it proved to be difficult. Sweet cherry varieties don't pollinate themselves, so they need to be planted in a group in order that cross-pollination can take place. The sour cherry varieties do self-pollinate and therefore are easier to cultivate. Because cherry trees were hard to cultivate, they were 'domesticated' long after grapes and olives. Propagation can only be achieved by grafting, a practice that had been invented in China, and was unknown in Europe until the rise of the Greek and Roman civilisations.

As the Roman Empire declined, so it seems did the popularity of cherries. Then in the Middle Ages there was a revival and the cherry fairs were born.

The cherry became symbolic of the meaning of life itself. In the Middle Ages, country people across Europe regarded cherries as symbolic of the 'passing moment', the fleeting happiness of life, love and beauty. They were living in the shadow of the Black Death and their lives were dominated by religion. So, perhaps their slightly morbid celebration of the short cherry harvest is understandable. A lyric from the 15th Century ponders:

> "This life, I see, is but a cherry fair.
> All things pass, and so must I, in any case."

> If you think that's too morbid, consider a
> more up to date lyric:
> "Life is just a bowl of cherries,
> so live and laugh at it all!".

That comes from an old song exhorting listeners to forget about the hardships of life, forget about making money and worrying about work. You can't take it with you, the song says, enjoy it while you can. Cherries are seen in both lyrics as a very good way of illustrating what we might say these days – live for the day.

## Cherry revival

Henry VIII was instrumental in reviving cherry farming in England; he ordered the importing of cherry varieties from the Low Countries and the planting of them in Kent. In those far off days they knew that cherries were easy to preserve, either in jam or pickle, or perhaps with brandy. They also knew how to make cherry ale, using the cherries that were leftover or damaged, and I'm told this is still available in Kent in the season. They knew that cherries went very well with game and, of course, they were familiar with the fabled cherry pie. Henry's daughter, Queen Elizabeth, is widely credited with cooking the first cherry pie, although I don't imagine she actually cooked it herself! Pie in those days often meant an open pie in the French style, because the English court would have been heavily influenced by the more fashionable French court.

Of course, the best way to eat cherries has always been by the handful, fresh and sweet! And straight from the tree, or at least from a farm stall by the side of the road, as fresh as possible. Don't do as a workman in Wanstead did in 1752. He had a 'carpe diem' (seize the day) moment when he reached out and stole a cherry pie from a pie man passing the George Inn. He was arrested and brought before the magistrates who fined him half a guinea – about 52p nowadays but a considerable sum in 1752. Nevertheless, he seemed to have had a sense of humour, because he erected a stone tablet commemorating his misfortune.

The inscription reads:

> "In Memory of ye cherry pey
> As costs half a guinea
> ye 17 of July.
> That day we had good cheer
> I hope to so do for many a year."

That workman clearly understood the meaning of life and cherries!　●

# Cherry pie

Or Queen Elizabeth's cherry pie! It's an open pie more like a tart, the most traditional cherry dish, baked in this country for 500 years and celebrated in literature and song.

For the crust:
**300g (11oz) plain flour**
**150g (5oz) butter**
**2 eggs**
**Salt**
**3 tbsp very cold water**

For the filling:
**1.2 kg (2lb 10oz) pitted, sweet cherries (fresh or frozen)**
**150g (5oz) sugar**
**3 tbsp cornflour**
**Orange juice and fresh orange peel, grated**
**1 tsp ground cinnamon**
**Drop of almond essence**
**Salt**
**1 egg, beaten.**

## METHOD

First make the pastry. Cut the butter into pieces and rub the flour and butter together until the mixture looks like breadcrumbs. Add the eggs and a little water and, using a knife, mix together until you have a dough. Tip out onto a floured board and knead briefly. Wrap in cling film and put in a fridge for at least 30 minutes.

While the dough is chilling, prepare the filling. In a bowl, mix the sugar, the cornflour, two tablespoons of orange juice and one tablespoon of grated orange peel, one teaspoon of ground cinnamon, and add a dash of almond essence and a pinch of salt. Then add the cherries, tossing together. Put to one side for about 30 minutes.

Back to the pastry: grease a 225mm (9in) tart tin, divide the pastry into two halves, one a bit bigger than the other. Take the larger piece and, on a floured board, roll out the pastry until it is quite thin. Cut out a round to cover the tin, maybe 300mm (12in) or a bit larger.

Pre-heat your oven to 200ºC (400ºF, gas 6). Line your tart tin with the pastry round. Then take the second portion of dough and roll it out so that you have a rectangle about 300mm x 200mm (12in x 8in). You will be cutting out strips for a lattice top from this so use your eye and judge whether my measurements will fit your tart!

Using a pastry wheel or sharp knife, cut the rectangle lengthways into nine 18mm (half inch) strips.

Then back to the filling. Spoon the filling into the pastry case, place five strips across the tart in one direction and then the remaining four across in the other direction to form the lattice top. Press the ends into the edge of the pastry to seal together, crimp the edge all the way around and decorate if you wish.

Brush the pastry with an egg glaze, then sprinkle a little sugar over the top of the pie.

Place in the oven, and bake for about 20 minutes. Then use tinfoil to cover the edges of the crust and bake for another 40 minutes, until the pie is golden and the filling is bubbling.

Remove from the oven and allow to cool. Serve by itself or with cream. A medieval feast!

# Venison with cherries

Cherry sauce is a famed accompaniment to game dishes, or any cold meat. It's traditionally served with duck, but I thought I'd cook venison with sour cherries, a simple classic country meal. These days venison is on sale everywhere as people become more health conscious and realise the benefits of eating such a lean meat. I used a thick venison steak cut from the haunch.

1 venison steak per person

For the cherry sauce:
**300g (11oz) morello (sour) cherries – ideally fresh, but you can use tinned or frozen**
**1 small carrot**
**1 shallot**
**1 stick of celery**
**1 clove of garlic**
**Thyme or rosemary, a few fresh sprigs**
**Juniper berries**
**25g (1oz) butter**
**Red wine**
**Beef stock (from a cube will do)**
**Salt and fresh black pepper**
**1 tbsp redcurrant jelly, or cranberry sauce**

## METHOD

Heat a griddle pan – the ridged type is best - until it is smoking hot. Place the steaks on the griddle to sear for about three minutes, then reduce the heat slightly and cook for a further two to three minutes. Turn the steaks over and cook for another five to six minutes. If you like your meat rare then reduce the times by about three minutes, and if you like it well done (shame on you) then increase the time. Remove from the griddle and put on a plate, cover and leave to rest.

Make the sauce by putting the garlic, carrot, shallot, celery and herbs into a food processor, and whizz for a few seconds so that they are chopped but not made into a paste. Melt some butter in a pan, add the vegetables from the processor and then crush half a dozen juniper berries and throw them into the mix. Stirring, cook for a few minutes until they brown. Add two large glasses of the red wine and boil until the mixture reduces, then add the beef stock and the redcurrant jelly, and then the cherries.

Bring back to the boil and reduce the liquid by about half. Then strain the liquid into a bowl through a fine sieve. Tip the cherries out of the sieve and rub the remaining residue through the sieve into the liquid. This refines the sauce, removing any grittiness. Quickly clean your pan and then pour back the liquid and return the cherries to the mixture. Test for seasoning and adjust as necessary.

Serve the venison with mashed parsnips, a dish fit for a king!

# Clarissa's clafoutis

This is a firm favourite in my house, sometimes when we come home late from work and tired, I just make one of these instead of a meal. Perhaps a bowl of homemade soup and then the Clafoutis It is comfort food, but light and more-ish.

There are many variations of this dish, which was probably introduced to England by the Norman invaders.

**50g (2oz) butter, unsalted is better**
**Vanilla pod**
**6 eggs**
**225g (8oz) sugar**
**300ml (½ pint) milk**
**Kirsch, just enough to soak the cherries.**
**75g (3oz) plain flour**
**Salt**
**450g (1lb) stoned black cherries**

### METHOD

I usually work out the ingredients by eye and make my clafoutis in a heavy cast iron pan, something like a paella pan. Pre-heat the oven to 200°C (400°F, gas 6) and generously butter the pan. Soak the cherries in the Kirsch for about 15 minutes, remove and drain.

Put the eggs, sugar, milk, and the Kirsch left from soaking the cherries into a blender, and add a pinch of salt. Whizz for a few seconds and then add the flour, blending until smooth. Pour the mixture into the dish and scatter the cherries on top. Lay a vanilla pod in the middle. Place in your oven and bake for about 40 minutes. Remove, allow to cool slightly and serve.

# Panperdy

Panperdy is a corruption of Pain Perdu, which is French for 'lost bread'. This is a very old recipe going back to Roman times, and mentioned by the Roman writer Apicius and originally known in France as Pain ala Romaine, or Roman bread. Now mostly known as French Toast but found all over the world under different names and guises.

The beauty of this dish is the way it can be adapted by using either simple or exotic ingredients. Originally it was thought to have originated as a use for old and stale bread, and therefore the food of poor people. But, since it turns up in many cookery books down the centuries, it was probably a recipe for the richer members of the population, since cookery books were intended for the educated, moneyed classes. This is an easy pudding dish or midday snack. This recipe has been around in England for about 1000 years.

**450g (1lb) ripe cherries, stoned (Black cherries are best and fresh, but good quality tinned cherries will do)**
**4 slices of white bread, about 6-8mm (¼in) thick**
**300ml (½ pint) milk**
**45g (2oz) butter**
**Sugar**
**1 large egg**

### METHOD

Place the milk in a mixing bowl and beat in the egg with about 12g (½oz) of sugar.

Cut the slices of bread into two and then place them in the milk mixture to soak for about five minutes, moving them around from time to time.

Place the cherries in a saucepan with about 25g (1oz) sugar, and gently heat them up until they are not quite at boiling point. Reduce the heat so that the cherries stay hot, and meanwhile melt the butter in a frying pan until it is bubbling. Then place the bread slices in the pan and fry them, turning so as to fry on both sides.

Don't over do it, we're aiming for a crisp outer layer and a softer inner layer.

Place four of the slices onto a warm dish and then place a quarter of the cherries (drained) onto each slice. Then put the remaining slices on top.

Sprinkle sugar across the hot sandwiches and serve with the leftover cherry juice. Serve with cream, or ice cream.

Summer

# Lobster & Lettuce

## Clarissa Porter
goes on the trail, or should that be tail, of a literary dish

**W**atching Dickens' Bleak House on TV, I was struck by the character of Mr Guppy and the offer to his new friend, Mr Carstone, of a lunch of lobster and lettuce. In fact I think Mr Guppy mentioned that Dickensian sounding dish more than once in the TV adaptation. Intrigued, I skimmed through my copy, but could only find one reference, and that is when Mr Guppy is eating somewhere in the Old Street Road with his mother and they share a lobster and lettuce.

Because I'm a sucker for everything Dickensian, I researched this recipe and found it not at all what I was expecting. But not a disappointment either. Lobster and lettuce is much older than Dickens' time, and, to Mr Guppy, must have seemed a traditional dish.

People have the impression that lobster is exclusive and expensive. That was certainly the case when I was growing up but now many supermarkets stock lobsters, and for less than £10. They are small but even so, there must be a demand. And my local street market has several stalls selling piles of lobsters. Nevertheless, the notion prevails that they are 'special'. Once, like so many special dishes, they were part of everyday life, as Dickens testifies. But sometime, probably after the 1st World War, they became expensive and frivolous.

***William Pinney knows what he's talking about when its comes to lobsters***

Like all the best traditional food, they have been with us for thousands of years. They belong to that oldest off food categories, food that was noticed by our forebears, rather than discovered (like bread). Communities living in coastal areas survived largely on a diet of seafood: fish, shellfish, or crustaceans like lobsters and crabs. Archaeologists excavating 'middens', that is mounds of discarded shells, have found lobster shells from the prehistoric period. The Romans certainly ate lobsters in this country. And now we seem to be coming full circle and, while still considering lobster to be special, it's certainly no longer exclusive.

They have long been thought of as an aphrodisiac, and are a staple of candlelit suppers for lovers. Interestingly, although there are several lobster dishes attributed to individuals and events, such as Lobster Newburg and Lobster Thermidor, they usually turn out to be fairly simple methods of preparing and serving this seafood. However, in these health conscious times, Thermidor may not be to everyone's taste. The best way to eat lobster is the simplest: cold, freshly cooked, with the most basic of accompaniments and seasoning.

This isn't because they don't keep. Apparently, a cooked lobster, wrapped in a brine-soaked cloth and buried in the ground, will keep for three months, and this was how they were once stored. Most chefs will tell you they should be cooked alive and eaten straight away. The more squeamish among you will have problems killing a lobster, so maybe the answer is to buy them ready cooked, from a fishmonger, or a supermarket. But they won't taste quite as exquisite as those freshly killed and cooked.

Modern thinking is that they should be rendered comatose by being left in a freezer for at least two hours before being plunged into boiling water. Weigh first so you know how long to cook them. Fill your (large) saucepan with very salty water. If you can float an egg on the water, it is briny enough. Bring the water to the boil, and drop your lobster into it. Place a lid on your saucepan and weight it. Bring the water back to the boil and cook for about 15 minutes for the first 450g (1lb), then 10 minutes for each subsequent 450g (1lb). The lobster will change colour from bluish to that typical brilliant pinky red. Remove, drain and allow to cool.

Some chefs say you should cut them in half while they are still alive and then cook. The jury is out on whether this is cruel or not, but I couldn't do it. A different method is to kill them by placing a strong knife across the section just below the head and hitting it with a rolling pin or mallet. The lobster will be killed instantly but will still wriggle. If it helps, don't forget that the lobster is a vicious creature, quite happy to eat each other, and even their own children, and they pick fights wherever they can. That is why you see live lobsters for sale with their claws firmly taped shut. Most of the lobsters in supermarkets will have been imported from places like Canada and Nova Scotia, and perhaps Scandinavia, but I think the British lobster has the best taste.

They are caught in traps called 'pots' and are easiest to catch in the summer when they are more lively. Lobsters in supermarkets tend to be on the small size, reflected in the price, but you really need bigger ones to enjoy them at their best.

Many people consider lobster to be the supreme seafood, even if they've never tasted it, which is a recognition of the caché of this strange, sweet-tasting creature.

A man who knows what he's talking about when it comes to lobsters is William Pinney. Not only does he own the Butley Orford Oysterage restaurant in Orford, Suffolk, but also the traditional oyster beds in nearby Butley, and the two smokehouses next to Butley Creek.

Orford is a sleepy backwater on the East coast There's a small castle, an old church, some pretty cottages, a village square and the restaurant. It has been in his family for more than 40 years. William's father, Richard Pinney, moved to Orford after the Second World War. At first he earned a living by cutting and weaving rushes. Then he restored the oyster beds, disused since the 1900s. Taking up fishing, he experimented with smoking the fish he caught. Then came the restaurant and, finally, the shop. They catch their fish and lobsters with their own boats, keeping the lobsters in tanks until they're needed. Visit www.butleyorfordoysterage.co.uk or, better still, make a real visit to this picturesque place.

Dickens probably knew the eateries around the Old Street Road (modern Old Street) in London, he may have known the Eagle pub, famous because of the nursery rhyme Pop goes the weasel, and the line: "up and down the city road, in and out of the Eagle". Somehow I can imagine Mr Guppy supping in there. I popped in the other day but, sadly, lobster was not on the menu. These days you are more likely to find burgers on menus in the Old Street area.

# Lobster tail parcels with Hollandaise sauce

A quick, impressive meal. Exquisitely pretty little parcels on a plate. Dishes like this are why lobster is considered elegant and special. Simple, like all the best recipes.

Serves 4

**4 lobster tails, weighing about 175g (6oz) each**
**50g (2oz) unsalted butter**
**Rock salt and freshly ground black pepper**
**4 squares of greaseproof paper, and some string**

For the Hollandaise sauce:
**120g (4½oz) unsalted butter**
**2 egg yolks from free range eggs**
**11/2 tbsp water**
**Juice of 1 lemon**
**Pepper and salt**

## METHOD
Pre-heat the oven to 220°C (425°F, gas7). Place each lobster tail on a square of greaseproof paper. The paper must be big enough to wrap around like a parcel. Place a piece of butter (12g/½oz) onto each tail. Season with pepper and salt. Wrap the tails in the paper like parcels, and tie with string. Place on a baking tray and put into oven for 20 minutes.

Meanwhile, to make the sauce, melt the butter in a little pan until just beginning to colour. Put everything else into a food processor and whizz until combined. With the motor still running, gradually pour in the melted butter, until you have a smooth emulsion. Taste the sauce and maybe adjust with more lemon, pepper or salt.

Serve each parcel on a plate with a warm bowl of the Hollandaise sauce.

# Lobster and lettuce

The dish from Bleak House, so beloved of Mr Guppy. I imagined it must have been a whole lobster with lettuce leaves – simple, up to date, and very 'gastro pub'. But it turned out to be quite different. Dickens loved to record the meals his characters ate in his stories. This one may have originated from America, which the author frequently visited to give public readings of his books. He lived during the period of the Civil War, and I found a version recorded from the Civil War period. Wouldn't it be nice if we could so easily find this dish in local hostelries today?

Serves 2

Meat from one medium (900g/2lb) lobster
11/2 tbsp of made mustard
150ml (¼ pint) vinegar
150ml (¼ pint) corn oil
5 hard-boiled egg yolks
Salt and pepper
2 round lettuces

## METHOD

Cut the meat of the lobster into small pieces, then shred the hearts of the lettuces, reserving the outer leaves. Mash the egg yolks, then combine them with the mustard, pepper and salt to taste, and the oil, so that you have a smooth paste. Mix this paste with the lobster and chopped lettuce. Serve with whole lettuce leaves and serve immediately with some fine tavern ale.

# Elizabeth David's lobster

The incomparable Elizabeth David championed everything seasonal and fresh, and managed to inspire cooks everywhere with her simple dishes. She clearly thought of lobster as special, and describes being on holiday and buying lobster from fishermen, tying their claws with her handkerchief, walking home and simply boiling her lobster and eating it with butter and salt.

This recipe is a little more elaborate but still has her unmistakable touch.

Serves 2-4

3 tbsp olive oil
8 spring onions, just the white stems, sliced (reserve the green part)
2 tomatoes, skinned and quartered
Dash of dry sherry
Lemon juice from 1 lemon
Salt and pepper
1 cooked lobster, meat removed

## METHOD

Warm the olive oil in a deep frying pan. Place the sliced spring onions in the oil and cook until soft. Add the tomatoes, salt and pepper, and let it bubble for a few minutes. Then add the sherry, let it all cook for a minute. Turn down the heat, add the lobster, cut into cubes, and let it all heat through. Add some of the green part of the spring onions, with a little lemon juice. Serve from the pan.

# Grilled lobster with herb butter

This is a classic way of presenting lobster – very colourful and simple.

Serves 4

2 lobsters, each weighing about 450g (1lb), pre-cooked and cut in half lengthways
50g (2oz) melted butter
Pepper & salt

Herb sauce:
110g (4oz) unsalted butter
2 cloves of garlic, crushed
Zest of 1 lemon
Small bunch of parsley, chopped and shredded
Small bunch of basil, chopped and shredded

## METHOD

Brush the lobster all over with the melted butter and season with pepper and salt. Place under a medium grill, shell side up first, and then flesh side up, for a total of 15 minutes. Meanwhile, melt the butter gently with the garlic, and keep on a gentle heat without burning the garlic. Remove from the heat, stir in the chopped herbs, and season with lemon zest, pepper and salt. Serve with a simple green salad.

**I** don't know why, but food always tastes better cooked outdoors. I've used a charcoal and wood fire to cook these recipes, making my own fire pit from large flat stones and utilising an old metal grill from an ancient gas stove as my grate.

If you are cooking in the country or on a beach, remember to always take the greatest of care. During the dry summer months it's all too easy to accidentally set fire to the grass. If you're using one of the store bought disposable barbecues you must not let the foil case come into direct contact with anything flammable, like grass! The heat from even a small BBQ is very intense. You will need to take aluminium foil and tongs with you, and maybe some heatproof gloves. Oh, and don't forget the matches!

And remember to always clear-up any mess you've made, and take it home with you! When in the countryside, as the Americans say: "Tread Lightly".

## OK, lecture over, cooking outdoors over an open fire is FUN!

Go on, build your own 'barbecue', dig a shallow hole in a beach, and line it with stones as I did. You may have a posh gas-fired barbecue at home, but it's time to re-connect with your inner Boy Scout!

You'll find that the impromptu barbecue has two heat settings: "very hot indeed", and, "warm". You use the former to cook your meat and fish, and the latter to warm the coffee pot, or roast vegetables in foil, or maybe fry bananas, that have been dipped in sugar, cinnamon and vanilla, as the sun goes down.

Look around your chosen picnic site, you may be able to find wild herbs such as fennel and thyme, I have found wild garlic growing on a sea wall near where I live.

Always use the best lump wood charcoal or briquettes. These can be 'flavoured' by adding aromatic wood chips, or if you've fruit trees in your garden, next time you prune them, store the cuttings for at least a year till they are well seasoned, and add them to your charcoal.

Marinades are an ideal way of preparing meat or fish for cooking over a fire, and they have the added advantage of preserving meat and fish on a hot day.

Once you have the appetite for cooking around a campfire, I hope you'll carry on into the autumn and even the winter. It is exhilarating and liberating to be free and outdoors, cooking and eating and enjoying life to the full! ●

# Outdoor Life

Nothing beats cooking over an open fire in the great outdoors. Whether it's a barbecue in your own back garden, or a portable barbecue taken to the beach, or a small gas stove for a country picnic, *Clarissa Porter* explains how

# Barbecue lamb anchovy, rosemary and lemon

I bet you've never tried anchovy with lamb!

This is almost a traditional barbecue dish. But my method is to cut the meat into large cubes, that way the meat isn't burnt to a crisp. I want your barbecues to be better than the usual sausage and burger affairs that blight an English summer!

Serves 4-6 people

**Leg of lamb, diced into large 5 cm cubes**

**1 tin of anchovies**
**Juice of 1 lemon**
**4 cloves of garlic, crushed**
**Olive oil**
**Fresh pepper**
**Fresh rosemary, lots!**
**6 wooden skewers, or 6 long woody rosemary twigs**

**METHOD**

I assume that you have lit your barbecue and it has reached maximum heat, the charcoal appearing white and ashen.

Squish together the garlic and anchovies in their oil in a pestle and mortar, add the lemon juice and some olive oil. Sprinkle some freshly ground pepper onto the mixture. This is your marinade. Toss the large cubes of lamb in the marinade and leave for about an hour. Then thread about three cubes of the lamb onto each skewer, and push sprigs of rosemary into the cubes, here and there.

Now barbecue! How long depends on you and your barbecue, and whether you like your lamb rare or well-done.

# Seabass with orange and fennel

My favourite fish... and just about the best fish to barbecue. This recipe is so simple and so good.

**1 seabass per person (about 450g/14oz each)**
**1 orange per seabass, 2 slices kept and the rest juiced**
**Fresh fennel, lots**
**Olive oil**
**Freshly ground black pepper**

### METHOD
Either buy your seabass gutted, or be prepared to gut them. Fishmongers will usually offer to descale seabass, but if you are barbecuing them, keep the scales.

Score the body of the fish three or four times, diagonally down both sides. Squeeze orange juice into the cavity of the fish, place a slice of orange into the cavity. Cut segments from the remaining slice and push into the cuts on the body of the fish. Stuff the cavity with lots of fresh fennel. Brush the fish with some olive oil on both sides.

Barbecue. Simple.

# Tomatoes with goat's cheese and geranium

This is a very quick dish, fragrant and deliciously colourful, an unexpectedly excellent dish to barbecue.

**Baby or cherry tomatoes on the vine**
**A few geranium leaves - not pelargonium!**
**Olive oil**
**Whole goat's cheese**
**Pepper and salt**

### METHOD
Place the tomatoes in a pan (how many depends on how many people and their love of tomatoes)

Nestle the goat's cheese (whole) in the middle of the beautifully red tomatoes.

Add some olive oil to the pan, and place on the barbecue. Sprinkle with pepper and salt. Cook till the tomatoes soften and their juices start to flow (so will yours) and the cheese will start to melt. This is the moment to add a few small fresh geranium leaves, and cook for about another minute.

Serve with fresh bread to soak up the tomato juices.

# Barbecued sticky pork with pears

Another taste surprise! Combining fruit with pork is of course a classic way of serving this popular meat. This recipe takes that a little bit further! Amaze your friends and make your barbecue something to remember

Serves 4-6 people

**Fillet or leg of pork, cut into large 5cm (2in) cubes**
**2 pears, quartered**
**A few dried prunes**
**2 cloves of garlic, crushed**

Marinade
**Fresh sage leaves**
**2 tablespoons of honey**
**2 tablespoons of grainy French mustard**
**Juice of 1 lemon, and the zest**
**Ground pepper**
**Olive oil**

## METHOD

Mix together the honey, mustard, a few torn sage leaves, lemon juice and zest and the crushed garlic. Add some olive oil, about four tablespoons, and some pepper.

This is your marinade. Toss the cubes of pork in the marinade, add the prunes (how many depends on your appreciation of prunes!) and then allow to soak for at least on hour.

Thread two or three cubes of pork onto each skewer, with some prunes and some of the quartered pears and a few sage leaves. Drizzle over a little of the marinade.

Barbecue! Since it is pork, turn each skewer and make sure the meat is cooked through.

Serve with new potatoes, you could cook these at home, then put them onto skewers and drizzle with olive oil and warm them on the barbecue.

# Three Summer Specials

**Clarissa Porter** serves up three quick and simple lovely starters or maybe lunches

These make ideal standbys for those unexpected summer visitors. You can make these in less than an hour, and impress your friends and guests with a twinkle in your eye and a chink of a glass!

There's a terrific terrine made from rough-cut pork and liver; a promising pate made from mushrooms with a dash of vermouth and lemon; and a classic British dish, the potted shrimp. ●

## Mushroom and Vermouth paté

You might think this an odd combination, but trust me, there's something pleasingly satisfying about spreading this delicious paté onto really special bread. I like to use large flat mushrooms, like field mushrooms. They have a sturdy meaty texture, and an authentic taste.

Serves 4

**2 shallots, finely chopped**
**2 cloves of garlic, chopped and crushed**
**25g (1oz) butter**
**450g (1lb) mushrooms, chopped finely**
**125g (4½oz) Ricotta cheese**
**1 tbsp Vermouth**
**Juice of one lemon, and a little grated zest**
**Fresh grated nutmeg**
**Pepper and salt, preferably both freshly grated**
**Chopped parsley**

**METHOD**
Melt the butter in a pan and add the finely chopped shallots and garlic. Fry gently until transparent. Add the mushrooms and cook for about 10 minutes until the mushrooms are tender and slightly mushy. Add the Vermouth, a squeeze of lemon, some lemon zest, the nutmeg and the salt and pepper. Taste, and adjust seasoning if necessary.
Put about three quarters of the mixture into a food processor and whizz briefly. Then fold in the remaining mixture by hand to add texture. Add the chopped parsley. Serve with olive or rosemary bread.

# Simple pork liver pate

This is, of course, a classic French country dish, one of the finest starters you could find anywhere. I like it for its lack of pretension and its enduring 'home made' appeal. Of course, in France they have endless variations, but the simplest is the best.

Serve 6-8

**450g (1lb) pigs liver**
**175g (6oz) pork belly**
**10 slices of streaky bacon**
**1 clove of garlic, crushed**
**10 peppercorns, crushed**
**2 tbsp brandy**
**Salt**

**METHOD**

Mince the liver and the pork belly, coarsely. Mix them together well and add seasoning. Leave to stand, for an hour if you can, and if you have time, overnight in a fridge. Line a one-pint terrine or loose-sided tin with the bacon rashers, try to arrange them attractively, and then spoon in the meat.

Place on a baking dish and fill half way up with hot water. Cover loosely with foil and bake for about an hour. Remove the foil for the final 10 minutes of cooking. Allow to cool.

Serve very cold with crusty bread and salad, and maybe a few gherkins and tomatoes.

# Potted shrimps

This has to be a classic British dish, but I wonder how many of you have tried it. It is so very simple, easy, quick and tasty, but somehow it has almost disappeared. And it's cheap to make, but expensive to buy ready-made, which I always think is a good reason for doing it yourself. That way you can make bigger portions, rather than the mean little pots you sometimes see in shops. Shrimps are the classic ingredient, but you could substitute crab or lobster. So off you go, and make sure you use shrimps, not prawns!

Serves 6

**450g (1lb) fresh shrimps**
**150g (5oz) clarified butter**
**2 tsp lemon juice, or anchovy essence**

**depending on ingredients**
**Pinch of mace**
**Pinch of cayenne pepper to taste**
**Nutmeg (optional)**
**Salt**

### METHOD

Preheat the oven to 180°C, (355°F, gas 4-5). If you bought raw shrimps, boil them for two minutes, but you probably bought cooked shrimps.

Peel the shrimps. Melt half of the butter and add the seasonings (use the anchovy essence with shrimps, and lemon juice with crab or lobster). Put the shrimps in an oven dish and pour over the butter with the seasoning. Bake for 20 minutes.

Remove and strain off the butter, putting it to one side. Pack the shrimps into smaller dishes, such as ramekins. Take the butter you have put aside from the cooking and pour over the shrimps in the pots. Leave them to cool and set.

Melt and clarify the remaining butter, and then pour over the dishes to form a buttery cover about 6mm thick. Try not get any air trapped beneath the butter.

Chill in a fridge, and serve with crisp lettuce, and thinly sliced toast.

# Strawberry field forever

Summer's here and so are the strawberries. *Clarissa Porter* tells you all you'll want to know

## Eton mess

Eton Mess is a classic, English dish for summer picnics. It's named after Eton School where it was traditionally served after the annual prize giving. Simple enough for you to transport the ingredients to your picnic site and then assemble when you arrive.

Serves 4 - 6

**450g (1lb) fresh strawberries**
**50g (2oz) vanilla caster sugar**
**350g (12oz) creme fraiche**

For the meringue:
**4 egg whites**
**Pinch of salt**
**225g (8oz) vanilla caster sugar**
**2 baking trays greased and covered with silicon paper**
**(Vanilla sugar is easily made by splitting a fresh vanilla pod and poking it into a jar of sugar, which it will permeate)**

### METHOD

To make the meringue, heat your oven to 110°C (225°F, ¼ gas). Whisk the egg whites together with a pinch of salt until stiff but not dry. Fold in half the sugar. Then beat in the rest of the sugar until smooth and shiny. Place even amounts of the mixture onto the baking trays. It doesn't matter too much about the size off the portions since the meringue will be crushed in the final dish. Bake for two hours until the meringue is dry and will lift easily off the paper. Remove from the oven and allow to cool.

Hull the strawberries and steep in the vanilla sugar for an hour in your fridge.

Then crush most of the strawberries so they are still recognisable. Crush the meringue into bite-size pieces. Quickly combine the strawberries and the creme fraiche. Pile everything into pretty glasses and top with whole strawberries and maybe a sprig of mint.

One of my happier memories is the summer I spent strawberry picking with my boyfriend. We were both at art school and with the summer holidays looming we saw an ad for strawberry pickers wanted in Norfolk. Brushing aside parental concerns we borrowed a tiny tent and two camp beds, bought a small camping stove, and packed it all into our Renault 4, along with the cat! We set off, confident the sun would shine… and it did. The camping area was ideally situated on the edge of the strawberry fields and the cat, intrigued by the nocturnal scrabblings of moles soon became accustomed to her strange surroundings.

We spent a carefree couple of weeks picking strawberries. There was no pressure to achieve a certain quota, you could pick as much or as little as you liked, and were paid by the basket. We were very happy, apart from the one night it did rain, when we discovered that the cat's habit of sitting on the ridge of the tent, sunning herself during the day, had led to a string of small holes appearing where she had clung to the canvas as she dozed!

All these years later, lying on the grass eating strawberries from a punnet, instantly transports me back to those happy, carefree student days.

We grow strawberries in our garden now, the wild variety, smaller and sweeter than some of the giants you see in shops and markets.

## Wild about strawberries

Wild strawberries are found all over the world. They ripen slightly earlier than the cultivated variety. Because of their shape and colour, wild strawberries have become part of the folklore in countries on both sides of the Atlantic. Most cultures have myths that involve plants: Jack and the beanstalk, for instance.

Strawberries have long been associated with nature and love, innocence, truth and virtue. In the French countryside, strawberries were considered an aphrodisiac, and newly weds would be given cold strawberry soup!

Native American Cherokee folklore tells that the Great Spirit created the first human being, a woman. Later he created a man to keep her company. At first they co-existed in peace, love and harmony, but then inevitably they quarrelled and the woman ran away towards the east. The Man was very sad, the Great Sprit heard his cries and told him to go after the Woman. The Man ran after her, but she had already travelled beyond his reach. The Great Spirit placed a patch of huckleberries in her way to slow her down, but she didn't stop. So he tried a patch of raspberries, and then blackberries. Nothing slowed her down. So the Great Spirit created a new berry, red and shaped like a heart. The woman stopped and tasted one, and found they were better than anything she had tasted before. She turned back to the west, remembering her partner. The man caught up with her, they made up, and they lived happily ever after. Native Americans call the strawberry the 'heart berry'. They were some of the first people to cultivate strawberries, mixing them with corn meal to make strawberry bread.

Unusually for such a delicious fruit, the Romans didn't seem very interested in strawberries. No mentions are found in the usual books, although the writer Pliny mentions fraga, the Latin name for the strawberry family, but he doesn't elaborate.

In early Europe there was a theory that strawberries shouldn't be picked and eaten because they grew low on the ground. Foraging for

# Strawberry and orange shortbread

My version of the North American classic, made there long before the explorers from Europe arrived. The open prairies of North America were carpeted with wild red strawberries. An early visitor, Lewis Mumford, described how horses' fetlocks seemed covered in blood from galloping across the plains!

Serves 4-6

For the shortbread:
**100g (4oz) butter**
**55g (2oz) caster sugar**
**Grated rind of 2 oranges**
**100g (4oz) plain flour**
**50g (2oz) cornmeal**

To decorate;
**225g (8oz) punnet of strawberries**
**Juice of the 2 oranges**
**Sugar to taste**
**300ml (½ pint) double cream**

**METHOD**
First hull the strawberries, then place them in a large bowl with the orange juice and a little sugar to taste. Place the bowl in your fridge.

Then make the shortbread. Heat your oven to 170°C (325°F, gas 3), blend the butter, sugar and orange zest together until creamy. Add the flour and cornmeal and blend until you have a smooth paste.

Place in a 15cm (6in) greased flan tin, pressing out with the back of your hand to fit. Prick with a fork and bake for 40 minutes. Remove from the oven and allow to cool for five minutes. Then remove from the tin a and place on a wire rack and allow to

cool. When cool place on a pretty plate, whip the cream and pile it on top, and arrange the strawberries on top of the cream. Serve!

wild strawberries was considered dangerous because of the possibility of encountering snakes. So the populace was discouraged from seeking out this delicious fruit.

Strawberries were being cultivated in South America long before explorers from Europe arrived. However, Charles V of France is recorded as planting more than 1000 strawberry plants in the Louvre gardens in the 14th century, the French being the foremost cultivators of strawberries in Europe.

But the real progress was being made in both North and South America, by the early settlers. It is hard to imagine today, but wild strawberries were once so plentiful that explorers would remark on the extent and huge amounts growing: "enough to fill a ship" wrote Londoner Roger Williams, the founder of Rhode Island in 1636.

He was a friend of the local Indian tribes and reported the Indian custom of making strawberry bread. In Europe, Louis 14th declared the strawberry to be his favourite fruit and instituted a poetry contest in its honour!

The modern cultivated strawberry originates from the chance crossing of a Chilean variety with a strawberry from Virginia. A French explorer in Chile noticed the large strawberries, and brought five specimens home to France, where they were planted in the Louvre and in Brest, which was thought to have a similar climate to Chile. They grew but produced no fruit until, 30 years later, by chance someone planted strawberries from Virginia in the same plot. This produced a variety known as the pineapple strawberry, because of its size. All of today's cultivated strawberries can be traced back to that chance union.

## Naming the strawberry

The name 'strawberry' has nothing to do with straw, although straw is used as an aid to cultivating this fruit. An old London street cry was 'Straws of Berries!' because they were sold strung together with straw. It is thought that straw part of their name originally meant 'strew', because they are most likely to propagate by sending out long tendrils, rather than by seeding themselves.

The Anglo Saxon name is streoberie. They are a member of the rose family, and are unique in having their seeds on the outside of the fruit.

And with summer here, one of the nicest ways to enjoy it is with a bowl of strawberries and cream. You might think that it's a recent invention, Victorian maybe, but strawberries and cream is a traditional and, perhaps, unbeaten way of enjoying strawberries at their best and freshest.

The happy conjunction of cream and strawberries is mentioned way back in the 16th century by Andrew Boorde, Doctor of Phisicke in his book The Brevery of Health. He wrote that strawberries with cream were a "rural man's blanket (comfort)", and went on, "I have known men jeopardise their lives for such a blanket". Perhaps an indication of the passions stirred up by this romantic fruit.

For me the appearance of English strawberries in the fields and shops is a sign that summer has truly arrived. This year I've decided to go to a local 'pick your own' farm for a day and recapture that happy Norfolk summer, but this time I'm going with my husband!  ●

# Minted strawberries

A simple but sophisticated summer treat. On a hot day the mint cools the strawberries and reminds you that strawberries are made in heaven!

**675g (1lb 8oz) strawberries**
**Stock syrup: 225g (8oz) sugar and 300ml (1/2 pint) water**
**Sprigs of mint**

**METHOD**
To make the stock syrup, dissolve the sugar in the water and boil for two minutes, then cool. Hull the strawberries, then take 225g (8oz) of them and crush. Combine the crushed strawberries with the syrup. Fold in the whole strawberries, strew with mint leaves, and chill.

Serve with sweetened yoghurt, cream, or creme fraiche, preferably sitting in your own strawberry patch feeling smug!

# Mint chocolate strawberry treasures

So simple, no real amounts needed here. You will have to judge how many you can eat.

Perfect strawberries
**1 or 2 bars of very good dark chocolate**
**Knob of unsalted butter**
**Slug of Creme de Menthe**

### METHOD
Melt the chocolate and the butter in a bowl, over a pan of hot water. Do not let the steam get into the chocolate. Pour in a little Creme de Menthe and stir until smooth.

Serve the chocolate in small bowls with mounds of fresh strawberries. Dip in!

## Strawberries have long been associated with nature and love, innocence, truth and virtue.

# The Wild Food Year Book

**F**ed up with processed, shop-bought foods? Want to make more of nature's bounty? You need The Wild Food Year Book – our guide to the best wild foods and an essential addition to any country cook's bookshelf. We'll tell you where to find the food, how to identify it and what to do with it, in a glut of unique and delicious recipes, writes Hannah Kilbey.

With full colour pictures and step-by-step guides illustrating the many different recipes, The Wild Food Year Book covers fruits and nuts, mushrooms, edible plants, rabbits, pigeons and game birds, sea, seashore and freshwater food, and explains the thrill of wild food gathering and why it benefits everyone.

If you enjoy cooking, but want to make food more fulfilling, then this is the book for you. It helps make meals special and really is the complete guide to using wild food.

- Fruits & nuts from the wild
- Woodland & field mushrooms
- Edible weeds and flowers
- Rabbits, pigeons and game birds
- Sea and seashore harvest
- Freshwater offerings

*Country* kitchen

Please make cheques payable to:
*Kelsey Publishing, and post to Kelsey Publishing Group, (WFYB)
Cudham Tithe Barn, Berry's Hill, Cudham, Kent TN16 3AG.*

## The Wild Food Year Book coupon

Please send me ............ copies of
*The Wild Food Year Book* at £9.99.
(Plus £2 p&p UK, £4 Europe/Ireland, £7RoW).

I enclose my cheque/postal order for

£............................ *(payable to Kelsey Publishing Ltd).*

Or debit my credit card:

Card No: .........................................................

Expiry Date:...................... Issue no: ...............

Signature: ......................................................

Name: ..............................................................

Address: ...........................................................

..........................................................................

..........................................................................

Tel: ...................................................................

Mobile: .............................................................

Email: ...............................................................

# Bring your holiday home

Your garden has everything you need to provide a tasty reminder of that wonderful holiday you've probably just returned from, here **Clarissa Porter** shows you how

**S**panish cooking is undoubtedly one of Europe's best-kept secrets, unsung and largely undiscovered in this country. Which is strange, given that Spain is still the favourite holiday destination for the British. But perhaps that is down to the fact that most holidaymakers insist on British food when they are abroad. The curse of the British 'all day breakfast' is alive and well on the Costas, along with 'chips with everything' and 'pizza'.

Which is a shame because cooking in Spain is almost by definition 'country cooking'. Even the smartest restaurants, in cities such as Madrid, Barcelona and Palma, serve dishes which are influenced by the heritage of a mostly rural population living off the land, or fishing for their supper in the warm Mediterranean or the wild seas of the Atlantic in the North. This has been influenced too by Spain's proximity to North Africa, particularly in the South of Spain where the Moorish influence is strongly evident in the food.

But the main difference between between us and the Spanish, and for that matter us and the French, is their passion for fresh seasonal produce. Food shopping is usually done in small neighbourhood shops or the local market, where tanned weather-beaten, happy people offer you their own freshly-grown produce. The eggs will be fresh and free range, the vegetables will not be blemish-free, and they will be dusty, but the tomatoes will be sweet and taste like tomatoes used to taste! The bread will be rustic and fresh from the oven, the olives will have been recently hanging from a tree, and the wine... well the wine will undoubtedly be rough, but it will be locally produced and taste all the better for that.

## Moorish is more-ish!

Spanish cooking is quite distinct from French cooking, which you might think strange given that they are neighbours, but Spanish cookery has been more heavily influenced by the Romans and the Arabs. The Spanish love sweet and sour sauces, and they love using fresh Mint, which is a taste they acquired from North Africa and the Middle East. Similarly, you find raisins and apricots being used in dishes with rice and salad, which is another Arabic custom.

The Spanish also have that delightful ritual of 'Tapas', little snacks such as chicken, ham, or fish croquettes. Bread and stuffed eggs, a little fried squid, and maybe pigeon and snails!

The ritual works like this, at lunch time, or before dinner, with a small group of friends, you wander from bar to bar, and at each stop have a small beer (and they are small) or a glass of wine or sherry, and help yourself to a selection of dishes arranged along the bar. Then indicate which dishes you've tasted, and pay what seems to be a piffingly small sum, then moving on down the calle to the next bar. And so on; no one seems to get drunk, and the conversation sparkles on into the night.

I've chosen four of my favourite Spanish recipes to hopefully help you recapture your holiday. The ingredients are easily found in this country indeed they could all be English recipes except for the peppers and the garlic. To a certain extent, all the countries of Western Europe share a common ancestry and have all been influenced by the Romans. Spain is unique with its North African connections, and all the more special for that!

Personally, I would find it difficult to decide whether France or Spain has the more interesting culinary heritage, I think my tummy says it is Spain!

Muy bien!

&bull;

# Broad beans with black pudding

This is a typical dish from the Spanish countryside, Catalonia in fact. But take a look at the ingredients, this is also very English.

If you live in the South of England, you may not have tried black pudding. But in the North, it is everyday fare.

Note that the Spanish normally cut their meat into smaller pieces than might be normal in this country. Broad beans are very Spanish, the staple diet for hundreds of years for people living in the countryside. Try to buy them freshly picked, you'll need to buy about three times the weight you want to end up cooking with, and shell them yourself!

Serves 4

**175g (6oz) belly of pork, remove the rind and dice**
**4 rashers of back bacon, also chopped into small pieces**
**175g (6oz) black pudding, sliced and halved or quartered**
**455g (1lb) broad beans, weight after shelling**
**Fresh mint**
**Olive oil, about 3 tablespoons**
**Sugar**
**Black pepper**
**White wine**

**METHOD**

Heat the olive oil in a large pan. Add the pork cubes, cook till they are golden, around 10mins, then add the bacon pieces and then the black pudding. Cook for another five minutes or so, everything will be sizzling.

Then add the broad beans, mint and a pinch of sugar and tip in a dash of white wine.

Add some salt if you like salt, but remember the bacon is salty. Season with black pepper. Stir gently and shake the pan about. Cook for about 6 to 10 minutes, you judge it is done.

Serve with more fresh mint and some bread to mop up the juices!

# Craddock's rabbit with hazelnut picada

I've dedicated this dish to some brave friends who've moved from London to an amazing 180 acres in Kent. There they grow hazelnuts (among other things) in glorious abundance, watched by an army of rabbits! When we visited recently we left with bags and bags of hazelnuts, so with memory of sun-bathing rabbits fresh in our minds, this old gypsy recipe from the heart of Spain seemed very apt indeed.

We buy our rabbits from a farmer on the Isle of Sheppey in Kent, they are of course wild, and they seem altogether nicer than the rather scrawny rabbits sometimes available from our local butcher. Picada just means minced or ground-up.

Serves 4-6

**2 rabbits, jointed into smallish pieces (you should be able to get 7 or 8 pieces from each rabbit). Save the livers and kidneys and hearts from the rabbits**
**Olive oil, a lot**
**8 tomatoes finely chopped**
**2 onions finely chopped**
**2 cloves of garlic, crushed**
**Parsley, chopped, about a handful**
**Plain flour**
**250ml ((8½floz) white wine**
**Salt and pepper**
**Thyme, fresh**
**Celery stick**
**Pinch of paprika**

For the picada:
**75g toasted hazelnuts (don't worry if you can't get fresh, they are available from your local supermarket)**
**3 cloves of garlic, chopped**
**4 pinches of saffron**
**Olive oil**
**2 red chilli peppers, chopped**
The cooked livers etc from the rabbits – cook them gently in a little olive oil beforehand.

## METHOD
Make the picada by taking all the ingredients, putting them in a blender and whizzing till they are a smooth paste. Then put to one side while you prepare the dish.

Using a large frying pan (or a paella pan!), fry the onions in some olive oil till they are translucent and golden. Add the tomatoes, garlic and parsley, and simmer till the whole is reduced to a thick sauce. Then put it aside for the moment. Toss the rabbit pieces in a little flour, and using another pan and some more olive oil, fry them till they are golden on all sides, but not cooked through. Then add the rabbit to the tomato sauce you have just made, add the parsley, thyme, white wine and everything else, except the picada.

Gently cook everything for about half an hour, or until you think the rabbit is cooked through. Remove the rabbit and arrange on a suitable dish. Add the picada to the tomato sauce, adding some water if you need to thin the mixture, stir and continue to cook for a couple of minutes, then spoon over the rabbit, and sprinkle the smallest amount of paprika over the dish.

Serve with salad and potatoes mashed with olive oil.

# Hake with potatoes and garlic

Hake is the quintessential Spanish fish. I have very fond memories of eating this dish in a small family restaurant perched on stilts in the middle of a bay, in a small village called Camp de Mar (which I think means 'farm by the sea'). It seemed that the whole restaurant was eating the same dish!

It is stunningly simple to prepare, if you can't find hake in your local fishmonger, then use cod or haddock, or even coley. Take care over the potatoes as well, too often they are tasteless and stale. The fresher the better!

Serves 4

**4 hake fillets, chunky if possible – or cod, haddock, coley**
**Olive oil**
**1 red or orange pepper, sliced into strips**
**1 yellow or green pepper, sliced into strips**
**1 onion, peeled and halved**
**1 stick of celery, halved**
**12 new potatoes, scraped and halved lengthways**
**4 cloves of garlic**
**Parsley, chopped**
**1 orange, take some finely grated zest, and squeeze the juice into a container**
**Salt**
**Paprika**
**1 lemon for garnish**
**METHOD**

Take two pans of water and bring them to the boil. One pan should be large enough to hold the fish without having to layer them. In other words, maybe a paella pan?!

Pour the orange juice over the fish, and put aside. Put half an onion and half a celery stick into each pan. Place the potatoes into one of the pans and add a pinch of salt. Cook them till they're tender.

When you think you are halfway through cooking the potatoes, put the peppers into the other pan and cook. Drain the potatoes, and keep warm. Put the fish into the pan with the peppers and poach for five minutes, or maybe a little less, until the fish is tender but not over-cooked.

Gently lift out the fish and drain. Then drain the peppers, discard the onions and celery. Arrange the fish on top of the potatoes and peppers on a serving dish. Quickly warm about six tablespoons of olive oil in a pan, adding the crushed garlic. Don't let it burn, remove from the heat and add the orange zest and paprika, stirring gently.

Spoon over the fish. Garnish with parsley and lemon wedges. A true taste of Spain!

Adios Amigos!

# Spanish eggs

This is a regular treat in the Porter household, easily made and a great brunch at weekends, or sometimes a warming supper when we're sitting on a freezing English beach pretending to ourselves that it's warm!

Serves 4

**4 large eggs**
**4 peppers, red and yellow preferably, sliced and chopped**
**1 red onion and 1 white onion, both sliced into rounds**
**2 cloves of garlic, crushed**
**8 tomatoes, halved**
**Olive oil**
**Thyme or rosemary**
**Sugar, salt and pepper**
**Half a loaf of stale white bread, crusts removed, cut into large cubes**
**Paprika**

## METHOD

Put the cubes of stale bread into a bowl and sprinkle some cold water over them – about half a cup – stir them around and put to one side.

Warm some olive oil in a large frying pan (funny how everything can be made in a paella pan!). Add the onions and garlic and cook gently till they are transparent. Add the peppers and cook for a few more minutes. Remove the onions and peppers, draining the oil, put somewhere warm. Put the tomatoes into the pan, sliced side down, and cook till they start to change colour, then turn them and season with salt and pepper, and add some rosemary or thyme. Now reintroduce the peppers and onions back into the pan. Keep on a very low heat.

Back to the bread: you are going to make 'Migas', the Spanish version of fried bread, but quite different from its English cousin. Drain the cubes of bread, sprinkle a little paprika over the cubes. Fry gently, don't try to rush them, slowly in a little olive oil till they are golden brown.

Now fry the eggs. While they are frying, arrange the peppers, tomatoes and onions on a serving dish. Place the fried eggs on top of the peppers, tomatoes and onions, then sprinkle the fried bread around the dish and serve.

The migas will be a surprise, instead of the crisp fried bread you're probably used to, they are like little doughnuts with a crisp shell. Once you've tried migas, there's no going back to the old ways!

# Classic cooking with a twist

The summer holidays are over once again. But before we start to look forward to autumn mists and the season of mellow fruitfulness, **Clarissa Porter** tries to recapture some of the tastes that so thrilled us while we were away in foreign climes

*"...what could be more British than a Sunday roast?..."*

**W**hy is it that dishes prepared in other European countries, such as France, manage to taste so differently to our own native recipes, while using basically the same ingredients. Is it that they use different quantities? Or do they cook for longer or shorter times? Maybe it is the subtle addition of herbs, such as garlic, that changes the overall taste to such a degree, that the food from a country becomes so indelibly linked to that country.

Anyhow, I'm sure that with a few exceptions, the ingredients are almost universal. Vegetables and fruit we might grow in our gardens or find in our local markets are mostly no different to those grown on the Continent. Indeed, these days most supermarket produce will have come from abroad.

At 'Country kitchen' we think fresh food freshly cooked is the aim we all have to strive for, and this is particularly easy at this time of the year, when our climate yields a harvest comparable to that available further south around the Mediterranean.

Some of you will have been on holiday abroad, perhaps in a rented cottage or villa, or on one of those brilliant campsites, and maybe you had to cook in an unfamiliar kitchen with just a few utensils and on a very simple stove. It is amazing what can be produced on just two gas rings powered by a gas bottle! And with luck, you had an oven! Though probably not if you were camping. And you will probably have shopped in a small cornershop or local market, trying to remember the few words of the language drummed into you at school, if you're like me, a good amount of miming will have been employed. To my mind this is the best environment in which to produce fine food.

But most of you probably stayed in a hotel or guesthouse, and hopefully you ventured out and tried the food in local cafes and restaurants, especially the local dishes.

So here are four recipes that will recapture your culinary adventures abroad, while still being honest country food, as much at home here as across the Channel. And what could be more British than a Sunday roast? In this country we have all the trimmings, vegetables galore, but this can be quite heavy on the tummy, and the poor cook preparing the meal.

In France they have a few tricks up their sleeves, which are well worth trying, and the meat dish is usually eaten in splendid isolation from the vegetables, which are few and simply prepared.

This can be rather nice at the end of the summer, when the weather is still warm and balmy. Simple is best.

●

# Roast chicken with garlic

This is so simple, and quite wonderful, a classic Provençal recipe which is at home here as it is abroad. Try this for a Sunday lunch, I think you'll agree it is simple but surprising.

Fly the flag and search out home grown garlic. Yes, it is possible don't you know that the Isle of Wight hosts an annual Garlic Festival?

When the garlic is roasted, it loses a great deal of the pungent effect on your breath. So don't be put off by what may seem an excessive amount of garlic. You can always munch Parsley afterwards to alleviate any lingering smells!

And use a free-range corn-fed chicken. If you've never tried a corn-fed bird, you'll be delighted at the subtle improvement in the taste. Serve with some bread, maybe a French stick, to soak up the juices, and instead of vegetables try a simple salad of Butterhead lettuce tossed in a little walnut or olive oil.

Serves 4-6

**1 medium size corn-fed chicken**
**1 kilo garlic (40 cloves is the minimum)**
**Lemon juice from 1 lemon**
**salt and pepper**
**bay leaves**
**fresh thyme**
**Olive oil**
**white wine, about a glass**

### METHOD

Take half the garlic, separate the cloves and peel. Put aside. With the other half, take a few bulbs and slice in half, the remainder, separate into cloves, peel some and leave some unpeeled. Season the chicken inside and out with salt and pepper, and squeeze the lemon juice over the bird. Stuff the bird with the garlic you have put aside, and with a bay leaf and some thyme, a few sprigs. Put the chicken into a frying pan with some olive oil, and fry gently for a few minutes to brown the chicken. Then put the chicken in the oven in a roasting tin, its best to put the bird in upside down. Roast for about half an hour.

Remove, turn the bird over, add the remaining garlic to the tin, with some olive oil, about half a cup. Roast for about and hour, you may feel it needs longer but remember you are cooking the garlic stuffing as well.

When you think it is cooked, remove from the tin place it on a serving plate with the cloves of garlic spread around the chicken. Add a glass of white wine to the juices in the roasting tin, let this cook for a few more moments add salt and pepper, and pour the juices over the chicken. Serve!

# Baked leg of lamb

This is the French way of cooking lamb, the French think they have kept this method to themselves, but, I have always cooked leg of lamb this way, having learned from my mother this "secret trick" way of ensuring the perfect roast lamb.

This dish is strictly speaking described as 'boulangere', which just means 'baked', the French don't usually say 'roast'. It is lamb with potatoes, cooked together in the same dish. One pot cooking at its finest, a recipe for another perfect Sunday roast.

Serves 4-6

**Leg of lamb, about 2 kilos (5lb)**
**1.5K (3lb) of potatoes, peeled and sliced**
**250g (8oz) onions, I used red onions, peeled and sliced**
**50g (2oz) butter**
**salt and pepper**
**Bouquet garni. You can buy ready made, but please make your own. If you can't, use a sprig of fresh rosemary instead.**

## METHOD

Put the leg of lamb in a large pan with about 2 tbsp of butter. Place the pan on top of your stove and brown the lamb on all sides. Then put the roasting dish in the oven pre heated to 230°C (450°F, gas 8) for about 10 minutes. Remove the pan from the oven, take the lamb out and stand in another pan for a moment. Using the original pan, soften the onions for a few minutes. Arrange the sliced potatoes and onions in the pan, add the bouquet garni or rosemary and season with salt and pepper. Pour boiling water into the pan so that the potatoes are not quite covered, then place the leg of lamb on top. Put back in the oven for about 40 minutes, then turn the oven off and let the meat carry on cooking for about another 15minutes. Carve and serve lamb and potatoes together. No need to make gravy, it has made itself in the pan! You really don't need anything else, but if you like, serve a separate dish of broad beans or a green salad.

# Quail (or pigeon) with green peas

This is another roast dish, but one that looks splendidly exotic. Strictly speaking, you should prepare this dish with pigeon, but I have a liking for quail. Quail are smaller than pigeons, so you will need to adjust quantities of birds either way. Actually, you could use poussin or duck legs, this is a very flexible recipe. Another 'one pot dish', and again very suited to the end of the summer, when a lunch outdoors may still be possible. I would serve with some bread to mop up the juices, and wine of course.

Serves 4

**1 or 2 quails per person (1 pigeon, duck leg, or poussin per person)**
**250g (8oz) smoked streaky bacon, chopped into small pieces**
**225g (8oz) small white onions or shallots, peeled**
**1tbs flour**
**750g to 1 kilo (1½lbs – 2lb) shelled fresh peas (fresh if possible)**
**Thyme, a few sprigs**
**Chicken stock (from a cube will do)**
**white wine**
**40g (1oz) butter**
**Oil**
**Salt and pepper**

## METHOD
Put the birds into a pan with the butter and oil and brown them on all sides. Then put them into a suitable ovenproof dish. Garnish the birds with strips of bacon and sprigs of thyme. Put the bacon pieces and the onions into the pan with the butter and oil and sauté until they are golden. Then put them in with the quails. Spoon the flour into the original pan with the butter and oil, add the chicken stock, a cup, and a glass of white wine. Stir, then pour over the birds. Add the peas, and season with salt and pepper, and more thyme. Place in a pre-heated oven at about 200°C (400°F, gas 6) for about half an hour if you're using quail, about 45 minutes if you're using pigeon, poussin, or duck legs. Remove from the oven when the birds are golden brown, remove any excess grease from the pan with a crust of bread. Serve by itself, there's no need for anything else.

# Upside-down apple pie (Tarte tartin)

We all love apple pie don't we? And this is certainly the season to be making them. In France, every little cafe, and every grand restaurant will offer Tarte Tartin. I make this dish all the year round, a classic recipe and like most classics, simple honest food. The only problem is stopping my husband from eating the whole pie in one go. Like all classics, cooks will make their own adjustments to the recipe, this is my version. You will need a tartin tin, usually a round metal dish with two handles, rather like a paella dish about 10cms -15cms in diameter. You could use a small frying pan with an ovenproof handle.

Serves 4 – 6 (or one husband)

**1 packet of ready-made puff pastry**
**1 kilo (2lb) Granny Smith apples, or similar, peeled, cored, halved, quartered and sliced, and placed into lemon water.**
**zest of one lemon.**
**110g (3½oz) butter**
**110g 3½oz) brown sugar**

## METHOD

Melt the butter and sugar in your pan on the hob. Add the apple slices, remember that this will be the top of the pie, so arrange carefully, you may want to arrange the slices in circles for a more fancy finished dish. Add the lemon zest. Place the dish on a high heat back on the hob. Cook for 5-7 minutes, the smell will change to a lovely caramelly apple perfume, and the apples will darken. This is essential. Watch this last step carefully. When this happens, remove from the heat and allow to cool for a few minutes. Roll out the pastry, and cover the dish, tucking any excess under like a blanket.

Put in the oven at 200°C (400°F, gas 6) for about 30 minutes. The pastry will rise and rise. Remove from the oven, cool for a few minutes. Then, carefully cover the cooking dish with your selected serving dish, and turn over so that your pie emerges right way up, apples on top. Serve with sweetened creme fraiche. The perfect pudding with any of the roasts.

# One potato, two potato...

**...three potato, more. *Clarissa Porter* just can't get enough of this vegetable that we take for granted**

## Irish Boxty

A traditional Irish recipe, said to have originated about the time of the famine. I've used Nadine potatoes, a second early cropped variety with a moist waxy texture.

The name comes from two Gaelic words meaning 'shelf' and 'fire', or so my Irish friend tells me! There is a traditional poem (of course) which goes:

Boxty on the griddle,
Boxty in the pan,
If you can't make a boxty,
You'll never get a man.

Serves 6+

**900g (2lb) Nadine potatoes, peeled and steamed**
**100g (4oz) butter**
**2 cloves of garlic, crushed**
**450g (1lb) self-raising flour**
**1 tbsp milk**
**Handful of sesame seeds**

### METHOD

Prepare two lined and greased baking trays. Preheat the oven to about 180°C (350°F, gas 4). Mash half the steamed potatoes until smooth. Coarsely grate the remaining potatoes, and pad dry with kitchen paper. Add the garlic, butter, flour, and the grated potato to the mash. Mix to a stiff dough. Knead briefly on a floured board and divide into two rounds. Place each on a baking tray, then press down the rounds until they have a thickness of about 25mm/1in (like a deep pizza). Score the top into sections like a cartwheel. Brush with milk and sprinkle on the sesame seeds. Bake for 20 minutes uncovered and then for a further 20 minutes, covered with foil. Serve with cheese, pears, ale and friends!

The humble potato has a long and interesting history, originating in central and southern America. So far, hundreds of species have been identified, from those growing wild in the Americas. One, the solanum jusepczukii, is the highest growing food plant in the world, or it was until 1995 when the Space Shuttle Columbia took a potato plant, solanum tuberosum, into space to see if it was affected by zero gravity!

So many varieties have been produced from these hundreds of species that no one knows for sure exactly how many varieties exist. What has been determined is that the original edible Solanum specie grew wild in the Andes region of South America. Some archaeologists claim that they were being eaten more than 13,000 years ago. They were certainly an essential part of the diet and survival of the Incas. It is not an exaggeration to say that the Inca civilisation was founded upon the humble potato. There are more than 1000 different names for the potato in the ancient Inca (Quechua) language, and the Inca unit of time was based on how long it took to cook a potato!

Spanish explorers to South America discovered these easily grown tubers in about 1537, in the region now known as Colombia. They took them back to Spain, thinking they were a type of truffle.

They were not a success; Sixteenth Century Europe had discovered the delights of the sweet potato and the artichoke. Early potatoes, in comparison, were bitter and watery.

## Part of the British diet

Potatoes were probably introduced to England during the 1560s. But no one knows for sure. Records do not distinguish between the sweet potato, discovered by Columbus in Haiti, and the potato. Popular legend has it that Francis Drake brought potatoes back from the Americas in 1586. Walter Raleigh had also travelled across the Atlantic, and he took potatoes to his estates in County Cork, where they flourished. The story goes that he presented some to Queen Elizabeth, but her cooks prepared the leaves and the green fruits for cooking, ignoring the tubers. This would have been almost inedible, poisonous even, and the Queen, understandably, was not amused!

As with many of today's popular fruit and vegetables originating in the Americas, potatoes then made the return passage – in 1621 crossing the Atlantic with the Pilgrim Fathers, and so being introduced to New England.

It was many years before the ordinary people of Britain began routinely eating potatoes as part of their everyday diet. All root vegetables were viewed with deep suspicion, and potatoes had the disadvantage of being related to the poisonous plant Deadly Nightshade. England was fiercely Protestant in those days, and ordinary country folk looked to the Bible for information. Sadly there was no mention of potatoes in the Bible! A rumour grew that potatoes were a Catholic invention, introduced to these shores by the European Catholics in order to subdue the Protestants and cause leprosy!

In those days potatoes were difficult to cultivate, producing their knobbly tubers late in the year in about November, if they produced any tubers at all.

But in the rest of Europe, by the end of the 18th century, varieties had been refined that flowered earlier, and by careful crossbreeding the previously knobbly tubers were transforming into the smoother tubers we know today. A French army officer, Antoine Parmentier, who had survived on a diet of potatoes as a prisoner in Prussia, persuaded King Louis XVI to try them. The King and his Queen, Marie Antoinette, enthusiastically adopted the new passion for potatoes.

The potato flower was used to decorate dresses worn by Marie Antoinette, and Louis XVI wore the flower on his lapels.

After the French Revolution, the Tuilleries Gardens in Paris became one large potato patch. It had taken more than two centuries of breeding and careful husbandry to produce varieties that would flower in the spring and produce tubers in the summer. By the early Nineteenth Century, it was reported that the English working man's main meal consisted entirely of potatoes.

Over in Ireland, the impoverished Catholic population had welcomed the potato. Ordinary Irish people lived in extreme hardship as a result of exploitation by absentee English landlords. Potatoes were easy to grow and could be stored for up to a year. Seed potatoes were passed from family to family, so the national crop became the result of inbreeding on a massive scale, which increased the potato's susceptibility to disease and blight.

Unfortunately this reliance on the potato was to prove fatal for many of the population, a population that had doubled in size to about eight million in less than a century. About one third of the population lived in such extremes of

# Forager's mushroom and potato

This is one of my favourite Elizabeth David recipes. Maris Peer potatoes would not have been generally available at the time she was writing but I think she would have approved of their superb flavour and consistency (and beautiful purple flowers). Excellent potatoes combined with large field mushrooms make for a peculiarly English dish. Elizabeth David emphasised the importance of being able to rustle up interesting meals without too much effort. This is one of my favourite lunchtime treats. It is especially nice to quickly bring it all together and wander into the garden and let everyone help themselves, straight from the pan.

Serves 4

**450g (1lb) potatoes (Maris Peer or Maris Piper, peeled and thinly sliced)**
**225g (8oz) field mushrooms, sliced (more if you like mushrooms!)**

**1 small onion, chopped**
**1 clove garlic, crushed**
**25g (1oz) butter**
**Olive oil**
**Zest and juice of 1 lemon**
**Chopped parsley**
**Tin of anchovies**
**Pepper and salt**

**METHOD**
Cut the potatoes into thin slices. Heat a little oil and butter in a large frying pan. Sauté the onions and garlic until golden. Add the potatoes and cook very slowly for 10 minutes. The effect is to simmer them very slowly in the olive oil. Then add the clean, sliced mushrooms. Season with pepper and salt.

Cover, and cook gently until the potatoes are tender. Then add the parsley and lemon juice, throw on the tin of anchovies, oil and all.

Serve straight from the pan! A delicious late morning brunch!

poverty by the mid-Nineteenth Century that it is estimated that in 1845 an adult male consumed 10-12lbs of potatoes per day. In that year a fungal blight spread across Europe.

In 1845 at the beginning of the famine, 2.5 million acres of Irish soil was used for potato growing. By the following year this had fallen to 1 million acres, and in the third year, 1847, this had shrunk to just a quarter of a million acres. This was a disaster. More than 1.5 million people died and over a million emigrated to North America. Diseases such as scurvy and cholera were rife, the Irish getting their vitamins from potatoes. Potatoes rotted in the ground and stores of harvested potatoes turning into stinking wet puddles.

The fungal blight hit Ireland the hardest and affected the Irish nation profoundly. But the rest of Europe was affected as well; the ferocity of the devastation has been compared to Black Death. But production revived in the second part of the Nineteenth Century, and potatoes became, along with wheat, maize, and rice, a major world crop.

Today, the world leader of potato production is China, and the biggest producers of potatoes in Europe are Russia and Poland. In this country we take potatoes for granted, but elsewhere the crop is of national importance. My Polish friend, Joanna, told me how as a young teenager, if a plague of Colarado Beetles was expected, children from her school and all of the neighbouring schools would be taken to nearby beaches, where they'd walk along the beach four abreast collecting beetles that had arrived on the waves, throwing them into fires placed along the beach. They would do this for at least a week, until the beetles stopped arriving.

The potato crop is of immense importance to countries such as Poland, but I can remember as a child seeing posters in libraries and public places urging us to report sightings of Colarado Beetles!

Next time you're in your local shop or supermarket, count how many varieties they stock. Too often the potatoes on display are just 'reds','whites' or 'new', and they may have travelled from Egypt or Israel. Even the organic offerings in my local superstore are from the Middle East.

We have become used to the ordinary spud. Bought for a purpose, chipping or baking maybe, or mashed, or in salads. But without any expectation of taste. Elizabeth David lamented that for a nation that produced and ate so many potatoes, we seemed so very unconcerned with their taste. Her answer to this conundrum was to grow your own. There are about 500 varieties available for you to grow, 500! It may be stating the obvious but different potatoes taste differently, and the soil they are sown in also affects their flavour. If you grow your own you ensure a plentiful supply of potatoes with flavour, not just texture. And, as someone once said: 'potato snobbery will keep you in touch with the seasons'.

## Season for second earlies

There are three main cropping periods: 'Earlies', 'Second Earlies', and 'Main Crop'. At this time of the year we are midway, in the 'second earlies' cropping period. Typical potato varieties from this crop will be 'Anya', 'Cosmos', 'Edzell Blue', 'Estima', 'Kestrel', 'Marfona', 'Maris Peer', 'Nadine', 'Saxon', and 'Wilja'.

# Dill and potato salad

What a treat this is! Pretty, colourful and light, just right for outdoors eating. Perfect with any marinated fish, such as my husband's favourite, rollmops. I've used Pink Fir Apple potatoes, these are either second earlies or main crop. I like to think that they look more like potatoes used to look, before they became uniform in shape. Misshapen knobbly tubers are not to everyone's taste! Pink skinned and with waxy yellow flesh, they are excellent in salads, but are good roasted as well. Once upon a time, the potato would let down a simple salad such as this. Thank goodness times are changing for the better and interesting potatoes are making a comeback!

Serves 4-6

**1kg (2lb 3oz) Pink Fir apples, steamed and cut into small pieces**

**1 red onion, thinly sliced**
**2 tbsp white wine vinegar**
**125ml (4fl oz) olive oil**
**½ tsp sugar**
**1 tsp Dijon mustard**
**2 tbsp sour cream, or creme fraiche**
**1 tbsp capers, drained**
**8-10 baby gherkins**
**Handful of chopped dill**
**Handful of chopped parsley**
**1 rollmop per person**

### METHOD

Combine the olive oil, sugar, vinegar, mustard and cream. Gently combine with the onions, potatoes, gherkins and herbs. Top each serving with a rollmop. Serve with slices of rye bread.

If you don't like rollmops you could substitute peppered mackerel or smoked salmon.

## "The Inca unit of time was based on how long it took to cook a potato!"

There's a good chance you've never seen or heard of any of them! But don't take that as a criticism, instead take it as a challenge, make a list and head out to the nearest farm shop or market and ask for them. I was in a farm shop recently and the only potatoes displayed were King Edward's and Maris Piper. Both varieties from the main crop season, therefore they had been stored since the previous year. They were in excellent condition, but it would have been nice to see some potatoes that had just been pulled from the ground. I'm afraid this is where we are all going wrong, buying potatoes almost without thought or care. We no longer notice that they are flavourless.

Take the chip as presented to us by a fast food restaurant, or 'french fry' as they call it. (By the way it is likely that the French actually did invent the chip, at the end of the Nineteenth Century street vendors in Paris were selling 'pommes Pont Neuf', crescent-shaped slices fried in lard). Don't you think they have a strange, chemical after taste? Maybe it's just me, but chips 'with everything' is an overworked culinary cliché. I don't want my chips to taste of vinegar or gravy. Why shouldn't chips be tasty on their own? It is probably something to do with the oil. Anthony Bourdain says you should use peanut oil, but Rick Stein extols the virtue of frying in beef dripping, which is the old way but not practicable for today's cooks.

Chips were first mentioned in an English cookery book called Shilling Cookery, published in London in 1854, and of course 'French Fry' is nothing to do with the country, but a description of the 'Julienne' method of cutting vegetables into strips. The Americans found it difficult to pronounce, so they called them 'French Fried', and then 'French Fry'. I expect everyone knows how crisps were invented. The story goes that a diner in a restaurant in Saratoga sent his french fries back, saying they were too thick. The chef, George Crum, was so annoyed by this that he sliced some potatoes extra thin and fried them till they were hard. He sent them back to the diner and was astounded to be hailed as a culinary genius!

Here in Britain chips are a national institution. During the Second World War, fish and chips were specifically excluded from rationing.

In my search for somewhere to buy 'real' potatoes, I stumbled across The Potato Shop at Morghew Organic, near Tenterden in Kent. Founded by Tom Lewis in 2001, it currently produces 22 varieties of potato. Selling from farmers markets across southern England, its philosophy is 'local, local, local'!

If you are fortunate enough to be nearby, The Potato Shop operates an honesty stall, open every day from 8am-8pm. If you need any potatoey advice I'm sure they won't mind if you give them a ring: 01580 766866, or contact them via www.thepotatoshop.com

One final thought on this immense subject. Those Spanish explorers conquered and destroyed the Inca civilisation in their quest for gold but they unwittingly gave the world something far more valuable to ordinary people, the potato!

*And 'spud'? Well, spud is the name given to the short spade that was used to pull potatoes – originally a word for a dagger!*

# Upside down potato tart

This is a main course version of one of my favourite puddings, the Tarte Tartin.

You could use Charlotte potatoes, Nicola, or Maris Peer varieties, or Pink Fir again – varieties that don't disintegrate when cooked. Using potatoes with apples manages to combine sweet and savoury tastes in an unexpected way. Adding Cheddar cheese makes it a firm favourite with my friends' children. Potatoes are naturally sweet remember. High in starch, the starch converts to sugar the longer the potatoes are stored. Hence their suitability for distilling into vodka or the Irish spirit, poteen!

Serves 4-6

**450g (1lb) potatoes, steamed or boiled until tender**
**2 Granny Smith apples, sliced into slim crescents**
**1 large red onion, peeled and sliced into rounds**
**Olive oil**
**1 clove of garlic, crushed**
**Salt and pepper**
**50g (2oz) sugar**
**50g (2oz) butter**
**Zest of a lemon**
**Sprigs of rosemary or thyme**
**125g (4½oz) strong Cheddar cheese (you could use a different cheese)**

**Packet of puff pastry, rolled out thinly so that it is slightly larger than the pan you will use**

### METHOD

Drain the potatoes, and slice crossways across their lengths, into two or three pieces. Using a frying pan with a metal handle, or ovenproof dish, or tarte tartin dish, about 23cm (9in) diameter: sauté the onion and garlic in the olive oil until transparent. Melt the butter in the same pan and add the sugar. Add the sliced apples, seasoned with pepper, salt, and lemon zest. Cook for a few minutes until the butter begins to smell of caramel.

Carefully remove the apples and onion with a slotted spoon and put to one side. Place the sprigs of herbs in the pan, and arrange the potatoes attractively in the pan (this will be the top of the tart at the finish). Next, arrange the apples and onions on top of the potatoes and sprinkle with the cheese. Place the rolled out pastry on top and tuck the excess in the sides.

Bake for 25 minutes at 200°C (400°F, gas 6), then reduce the heat and bake for a further 15 minutes at 180°C (350°F, gas 4) until the pastry has really puffed up and is golden. Remove from the oven and allow to cool for a few minutes, then place your serving plate over the top of the pan (oven gloves please) and carefully invert.

Serve, warm and gooey with a glass of cold cider!

Autumn

# Hunter's sandwich

Tradition has it that huntsmen (and women!) carried a sandwich of bread and steak with them on their adventures, says **Clarissa Porter**

# Hunter's sandwich

This is the original and probably best version. The problem is that it is difficult not to personalise the recipe, so what follows is not a definitive recipe. Please think creatively and add ingredients you may like, such as mustard, or chillies, garlic or onions. Or leave out the mushrooms and just have steak!

This is not the sort of recipe that has to be followed slavishly.

**1 white loaf, small medium or large
depending on needs
750g (1½lb) Steak,
(I used sirloin, enough to fill loaf)
3 or more Portabella mushrooms, peeled
and sliced
salt and pepper**

**METHOD**
Cut the end off your loaf, remove most of the centre. Season your steak with pepper to taste. Do not use salt at this stage, or it will draw the juices out of the steak.

Grill or fry your steak, I think it is best to undercook it. When it has been cooked you can add salt. Fry or grill the mushrooms. Stuff the loaf with the steak and mushrooms, steak in the middle surrounded by the mushrooms. Any gaps can be filled with the bread crumbs soaked in the juices from the cooking. Replace the cut-off end of the loaf. Wrap in greaseproof paper and tie with string. Wrap more greaseproof or kitchen foil around the parcel. Place somewhere cool and put a board on top. Then place a weight on top, bags of flour or sugar make good weights. Leave for 6 hours, or even overnight.

Your sandwich is ready for anything, when you're hungry, slice like a loaf and eat. You could find yourself having a beer at the same time maybe!

**N**ow this is certainly true, up to a point. But, I don't believe they were the sort of hunters that wore pink, and who can still be seen chasing around the countryside on horseback after packs of hounds. No, I think they were more likely to have been solitary hunters, poachers even! Maybe two or three friends out for the chase, on foot or horseback. Looking for game, furred and feathered, and finned. Food for the pot, hunted with lurchers, ferrets, rods and guns.

Neither was it a sandwich in the accepted sense, resembling more a large cold bread pie, designed to carry and contain a sustaining meal of meat, and to stay appetising for a hunting trip lasting several days. Actually, it was intended to be eaten the day after it was made, unlike a conventional sandwich!

Also known as a Shooter's Sandwich, this delicious and unusual countryside dish has been enjoyed for at least 300 years in this country, and it is also enjoyed in the backwoods of America, and as far afield as the Australian Outback.

I think the word 'sturdy' best sums up this dish. Outdoorsy and wild, something to put in the bottom of your shooting bag, with all your hunting gear piled on top of the sandwich. Good basic food for serious hunters, people who plan to eat what they catch.

For those of us that don't hunt, the Hunters Sandwich makes excellent picnic food, or food for a journey.

When hunger strikes, cut off a slice and settle back, surely this is what makes life worth living!

We start with the classic recipe, and then I've added a couple of alternatives. This is such a lovely simple dish, and very adaptable to your own taste. I suggest you experiment with different loaves, and vary the ingredients to suit yourselves.

Some loaves lend themselves better than others to the method.

So here are three very different 'sandwiches', remember make them the day before, then off to the hills!

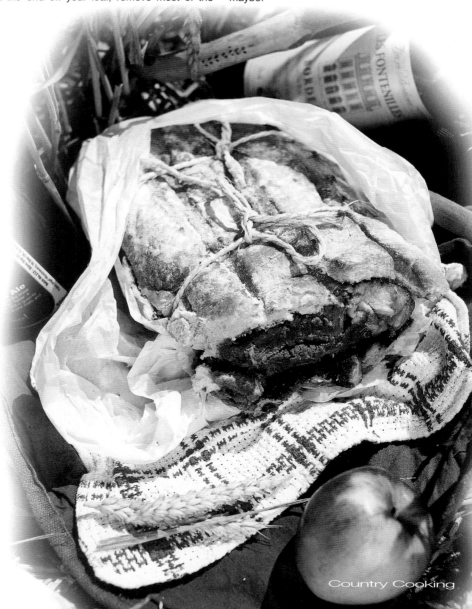

# Poacher's sausage sandwich

My own variation on the classic Hunters Sandwich. I couldn't resist making it a bit more complicated, sorry! This will take a bit longer preparing, but the result will be worth it.

**1 round white loaf**
**450g (14oz) sausages (I used a continuous spiral sausage)**
**Olive oil**
**Onion marmalade**

### METHOD

Cut your round loaf across lengthways, like a hamburger bun, leave a small section uncut like a hinge. Scoop out some of the centre, so that each half resembles a shell. Save the bread for breadcrumbs. Fry the sausage in a little oil till its golden. Next put a generous portion of the onion marmalade into the bottom half of your loaf. Place your sausage on top of the onion marmalade, and close the bread 'lid'. Press down hard, and tie with string. Wrap in greaseproof paper and tie with more string. Place a board on top of the loaf, and weight it with something heavy. Leave preferably overnight. When hungry, slice like a cake and enjoy!

**Onion marmalade**
**1.5k (3lb) red onions, sliced**
**6tbs white wine vinegar, or balsamic vinegar**
**3tbs olive oil**
**125g (4oz) brown sugar**
**salt and pepper**

### Method

Heat some oil in a heavy pan, add everything except the vinegar. Cover and allow the onions to brown, stirring from time to time. Cook for about 30 minutes. Then add the vinegar, and continue to cook for a few more minutes. Remove from the heat and allow to cool. There will be enough for your sandwich, and some left over top save for another day.

# Bread soaked in oil (Pan Bagna)

This is a continental version, beloved of French hunters and I'm told, boules players, particularly in the hot South of France. I believe the name refers to, or means, a 'bread bath', because of the soaking in salt water and olive oil! So, whereas the previous two sandwiches were dry and meaty, the Pan Bagna is decidedly damp! Which can be very refreshing if you manage to keep it cold on your travels. I think it is really delicious, and perhaps easier to prepare than the other two sandwiches. It adapts very well to this country, and I include it because it provides a vegetarian alternative (depending on your view of anchovies) to the determinedly meatier versions.

Serves 4

**1 baguette (French loaf)**
**1 small tin of anchovies in oil**
**50g (1oz) mushrooms, cooked in water with olive oil, bay, thyme,** coriander seeds, and pepper. Drain and cool
**1 artichoke (tinned)**
**100g (3oz) black olives**
**225g (6oz) tomatoes, sliced**
**1 celery heart (tinned), cut into strips**
**olive oil**

### METHOD

Cut the French loaf lengthways, completely in half. Soak each half in a little lightly salted water, then rub each half with a little olive oil. Put the sliced tomatoes, pieces of the artichoke heart, slices of mushroom, strips of the celery heart, stoned black olives, and several anchovy fillets into one half of the loaf. Replace the other half of the loaf, tie with string, wrap with greaseproof paper, tie with more string. Place a board on top, and then weights on top. Leave for at least 1 hour. Serve cut in to thick slices, with maybe some red wine and some crisp cheese.

# Fair game

**Clarissa Porter** follows her primal instincts and cooks up meals fit for a king

# Roast grouse

The Red Grouse is an excellent game bird, revered and almost a cult in hunting circles. The 12th August is the most important date on a huntsman's calendar. Because of their diet, grouse make a very delicious meal. A grouse can fly at 90mph and is definitely not an easy target!

Serves 4

**4 grouse, oven ready, livers reserved**
**4 slices of streaky bacon**
**50g (2oz) butter**
**Sprigs of fresh thyme**
**Olive oil**
**Salt and pepper**

For the pate:
**Dash of brandy**
**Dash of double cream**
**Reserved livers**
**Pepper and salt**
**4 slices of fried bread**
**Breadcrumbs from 1 slice of fresh bread**

For the gravy:
**Chicken stock**
**Dash of brandy**
**Dash of raspberry vinegar**
**Salt and pepper**

### METHOD
Heat the oven to 220°C (425°F, gas 7), season the birds inside and out. Place a sprig of thyme inside each bird, and a slice of bacon on top. Drizzle with olive oil and roast for about 20 minutes.

Remove from the pan and keep the birds warm. Scoop out the fat from the pan into a small saucepan. Fry the livers in the fat, smashing them as they cook. Remove, and reserve. Fry the breadcrumbs in the remainder of the fat until crispy. Now mash the livers with a little cream and brandy. Season with pepper and spread onto small triangles of fried bread.

Make the gravy by warming the rest of the juices in the roasting tin until quite hot. Pour in a slug of brandy and a little raspberry vinegar, and scrape the bottom of the pan. Now add a little chicken stock and allow to bubble away for a few minutes. Taste and season if necessary. Serve the grouse surrounded by fried bread, watercress, drizzled with gravy and scattered with the breadcrumbs. Nothing to grouse about with this dish!

From the stories painted in caves more than 30,000 years ago of people hunting deer and bison with spears, we know that game birds and animals are the oldest forms of meat eaten by humans. I know I always bang on about reconnecting with your inner caveman, but by eating 'quarry', which is almost by definition 'wild' food, surely we are doing just that. And the health benefits are inescapable, game being leaner and the ultimate in free range. Free range game birds just have to be better for you than the poor supermarket chicken who spends her life confined, standardised, and dosed with who knows what? Unfortunately I've not had the experience of attending an organised 'shoot', or of stalking deer. Not for me the pleasure of hiking across moorland slopes in the autumn and winter! But I know the excitement of unexpectedly disturbing a deer grazing in the woods or, as last weekend, driving down a narrow pot-holed lane on the Isle of Harty, the road ahead filled with brown hares 'boxing' and twizzling in the evening sun. What a mystical creature is the hare, blessed with extraordinary athleticism and a history of pre-Christian myth and witchcraft.

My hunter-gatherer instincts have been dulled by years of town living. But my neighbours are made of sterner stuff. They sold up and bought a farm in Kent, where the previous owners had run pheasant shoots. So my friends thought they would continue the shoots as a means of bringing in some revenue. But they only managed a couple of seasons. It is a highly organised endeavour. People pay a lot of money to shoot and expect to be catered for and looked after in every way. But the thing they tired of most quickly was cleaning and plucking dozens of birds after the shoot. Nowadays they just shoot for the pot, fun not profit. They introduced me to a very helpful game dealer, Necchi's, down a tiny lane in Kent.

Another Kentish game dealer is Phil Miles of Godmersham Game. If you've been to any game fairs in the south east, or the weekend market at Whitstable Harbour, you may have run into Phil. He sells game and products made from game, and very special they are too. I met him at the Kent Game Fair. My dog had just won 1st prize in the Lurcher Show and as a reward I went to Phil's stall to buy him a couple of rabbits. Phil waxed lyrically about how they'd been running around an orchard a few hours earlier, and how they'd make an excellent meal. Poor Phil, his face when I told him they were for my Lurcher! He clearly thought that he should be out catching his own rabbits and not swanning around with a large rosette pinned to his collar!

## What is game?

The loose definition of game is animals or birds that are 'quarry' and protected by law, usually wild or reared in conditions as near to 'wild' as possible. Grouse and deer are the main game ingredients. The 12th of August marks the beginning of the grouse-shooting season, 'the Glorious Twelfth'. Grouse is the ultimate game bird, protected and nurtured by gamekeepers across thousands of acres of moorland in the north of England and Scotland.

# Jugged hare

Boudicca is recorded to have released a hare from beneath her robes before her last battle with the Romans. This would have been a dramatic event, designed to bring victory. Unfortunately, the Britons lost!

Jugged Hare is a very ancient recipe, utilising a cooking method that just needed an open fire. Hares are normally jointed into five or six pieces. The front legs are known as 'wings'.

Serves 2-4
**1 hare, jointed. (Ask your butcher to do this, or cut your hare into 5 pieces)**
**125g (4½oz) fine oatmeal**
**Salt and pepper**
**A little butter**
**1 medium onion, peeled and stuck with two cloves**
**1 pear or apple, sliced**
**250g (9oz) peeled chestnuts (packet will do very well)**
**1 lemon, chopped into pieces**
**125g (4½oz) button mushrooms, sliced**
**Sprigs of thyme and parsley**
**Bay leaf**
**125ml (4fl oz) red wine**
**600ml (20fl oz) beef stock (from a cube will do)**

For the forcemeat balls:
**125g (4½oz) minced raw chicken**
**2 slices of bacon minced**
**1 onion, finely chopped**
**2 tsp parsley, finely chopped**
**2 tsp thyme, finely chopped**
**50g (2oz) fresh breadcrumbs**
**1 egg, beaten**
**Salt and pepper**
**Oil for frying**

For serving:
**Red currant jelly**
**Toast**

**METHOD**
Wipe the joints and season, then roll in some of the oatmeal and brown lightly in butter. Sprinkle the bottom of a large jug or casserole with oatmeal. (The jug should fit easily into a larger saucepan of simmering water.) Now place the browned joints into the jug. Add the onion, mushrooms, pear, chestnuts, lemon pieces, and herbs. Finally pour over the wine and the beef stock and any remaining oatmeal. Season with pepper and salt and cover with two layers of foil; tie with string. Place in a pan of simmering water for three hours. You may have to top up the water.

Towards the end of the cooking time, prepare the forcemeat balls. Combine all the ingredients and shape into 10 to 12 balls. Fry them until golden, in oil, for about five minutes.

To serve, remove the hare from the jug and place onto your serving dish. Strain the juices from the jug and pour over the hare. Retain the chestnuts and arrange around the hare with the forcemeat balls. Serve with toast and redcurrant jelly. History on a plate!

The only game available all year round are pigeon and rabbit. Hares are protected during their breeding season, so the hare season also starts in August. Game birds are: Black Grouse, Red Grouse, Ptarmigan, Partridges, Pheasants, Capercaillie, Snipe, and Woodcock. It is forbidden to shoot Quail at any time. Water birds (wildfowl) such as wild duck are also considered game. The rules are complicated and I recommend contacting the BASC (www.basc.org.uk) for information about shooting seasons before you set off hunting. Its website is a mine of information. Some of the laws relating to game and wildfowl date back more than 100 years, and there are variations from England to Scotland, and in some cases from county to county. But it is a definite no-no to shoot on Christmas Day or any Sunday!

There has been a trend in recent years to persuade us to eat more lean meat such as venison, and the increased demand has led to deer farming. Rabbits are also farmed, but on a very small scale. I recently bought a frozen rabbit in a farm shop, but when it was cooked the meat was as white as chicken. Farmed rabbit! This doesn't look right I thought, the rabbits I get from Harty Meats are dark and gamey. You'll have to decide for yourself the conundrum of whether or not it is right to rear birds in order to shoot them. This is one of those contradictions of modern life. I do know that the practice is very well established and traditional. Supporters would argue that the countryside and wildlife are preserved and enhanced by farms and shooting estates, and I am inclined to agree. The RSPB maintains an impressive neutrality on the subject. Game birds raised from chicks and cosseted by gamekeepers, and allowed to roam free are as wild as any bird, I think. The old perception of game hunters as a rich and privileged class has also changed, and more and more ordinary people are enjoying this sport.

## Seasons eatings

I expect the problem most people will have about eating game is the fixed dates of the open seasons. The 'I want some grouse and I want it now' consumer is going to be disappointed. Sorry, you'll have to wait until after the 12th August. In fact, you'll have to wait a bit longer than that because the other irksome problem with game is, with a couple of exceptions, that it needs to be hung. Wild rabbit, hare and venison should be hung for about three to 10 days, pheasants for at least seven days, and wild ducks for two or three days. Game should taste, well, gamey!

The price of rabbit, venison and pheasant is not exorbitant. I pay £2 each for rabbit, which is enough for two people. You shouldn't have any trouble getting hold of venison, pigeon or pheasant, although there are a few game dealers who specialise in mail order, via the web. I can recommend Dunstan Fish & Game in Cheshire (www.dunstangame.co.uk). It supplies oven-ready birds and smoked meats and will even smoke your own meat if you send it to them!

**More information**
Necchi's, tel: 01580 891602. Godmersham Game, tel: 01227 730337.

# Peppered venison with port wine sauce

Venison is the meat of royalty. Deer were the exclusive property of the titled classes. In medieval times, any peasant caught with one of the King's deer could expect a fearful punishment. The story goes that the dogs used for hunting deer were Greyhounds, the 'king of dogs, dog of Kings'. Common people were not permitted to keep Greyhounds, in order to prevent them poaching deer. And so the Lurcher came about by crossbreeding with Greyhounds. 'Lur' is Romany for 'thief'!

Serves 4

**500-750g (1lb 2oz-1lb 11oz) haunch joint of venison, sliced into 4 medallions (the joint will have been strung, so keep the string to hold the shape)**
**4 tbsp peppercorns, crushed**
**Butter**
**Olive oil**

For the sauce:
**1 glass of port wine or blackcurrant liqueur**
**125ml (4fl oz) chicken stock**
**1 tsp tomato purée**
**1 tbsp redcurrant jelly**
**Pepper**
**Knob of butter**

**METHOD**
In a large frying pan, melt the butter with a little olive oil. Wipe the venison medallions and gently press in the peppercorns on each side. Gently fry for a few minutes each side. Do not overcook, they should be pink like rare lamb. Remove and keep warm while you make the gravy.

Pour the port into the pan and scrape the residue from the bottom. Add the tomato purée, redcurrant jelly and the stock, and allow to bubble away for a few minutes. Finally add the knob of butter and whisk furiously!

I would serve the venison on a pile of mashed potato, surrounded by the port wine sauce.

# Store what you eat, eat what you store

**Clarissa Porter** reminisces about her student days when she would combine a few basic ingredients to dish up filling, economical and nutritious meals

I had a shock when I first left home. I'd rented a bedsit near to my college, leaving behind a comfortable family home with all the usual perks: free food, free heating, and free rent!

My parents thought if I was leaving, then I should stand on my own two feet. So support, financially anyway, was distinctly lacking. Nowhere was this more apparent than when it came to food. Students were really poor in those days, the idea of going down the pub, having a pizza delivered, or a Chinese takeaway would have been beyond our comprehension. Most of the week I existed hand to mouth. Breakfast was usually porridge, and sometimes porridge was dinner as well. The college had a cheap canteen, so lunch was a roll and a cup of tea. In the evenings I sometimes had a bag of chips, or when I was feeling like splashing out, a Vesta Chow Mein. This was a dry packet food, a bit like an early version of a Pot Noodle. We thought it was excitingly exotic.

The highlight of the week would be Monday, my boyfriend would return from the weekend carrying a large scrumptious bread pudding, sent by his mother. I'm telling you this story because, in a way the bread pudding is one of the quintessential store cupboard dishes. A lesson was learned that with a few simple cheap ingredients, a feast could be prepared. But having a store of these ingredients was the first step. So in my own hard-up way I began to assemble my first store cupboard. Soon I had concocted my own first store cupboard dish, the bacon and bean casserole.

This was a staggeringly popular dish with my fellow students. Two rashers of bacon chopped and fried, an onion sliced and fried, a tin or two of baked beans, mix them together with an Oxo cube in an oven proof dish, top with mashed potato (from a packet) and grated cheese. Heat in the oven and serve with a fried egg if funds allow.

Today, my store cupboard is the most important part of my kitchen. I grew up in houses that had built-in larders, large dark, cool and dry cupboards. But perhaps you think I am being a bit old-fashioned. Most modern kitchens don't have a larder as such, more a proliferation of cupboards, and shelves. I think it pays in the long run to arrange a special store cupboard, if you can. Somewhere cool, dry and dark, like a Victorian larder, to keep all those basic ingredients that you can fall back on in an emergency.

Before home refrigeration, and the coming of corner shops (and then supermarkets), clever cooks planned far ahead knowing that it would be all too easy to be caught out by events such as the weather, illness or shortages of one thing or another. They made their own preserves, and pickled onions, eggs, and walnuts. They were brought up reciting the nursery rhyme 'Old Mother Hubbard went to the cupboard...' certainly no one

# Lentil soup (or stew)

Friends pop round unexpectedly, and all you've got is a few vegetables lurking in the vegetable basket! With your store cupboard rustle up this warming thick soup. It is a meal in itself.

Serves 4
**1 small white cabbage, shredded**
**4 onions, sliced into rounds**
**6 cloves of garlic, crushed**
**50g (2oz) butter, or lard**
**2 tins of green lentils**
**tin of cooked chestnuts (250g/9oz) also available in long life shrink wrapped packets**
**large glass of red wine**
**thyme, large pinch**
**bay leaf**
**dash of lemon juice**
**salt and pepper**
**smoked sausage (optional, if you have them)**

**METHOD**
Melt the butter in a large saucepan. Add the onions and garlic and allow to soften.

Add the cabbage, wine and herbs. Allow to gently bubble away until the cabbage begins to soften and turns pink with the wine.

Add the tinned lentils, liquid as well. If possible add a little vegetable stock (from a cube). Add the tinned or packet cooked chestnuts.

Cook for another 5 minutes or so and then season with salt and pepper and a squeeze of lemon juice. The addition of a few slices of smoked sausage or bacon at this point will make this even more of a complete meal.

If you have time, remove from the heat, leave to stand for a while and then reheat.

Serve with crusty bread.

wanted a cupboard so bare that even the dog went hungry.

The notion of a store cupboard would have been a necessity in the countryside. You can easily imagine the need to store food at the end of the harvest to tide you over the Winter and into the following Spring. Nowadays the contents of a store cupboard may have changed, but the basic idea remains the same.

In the USA, keeping a store cupboard is still very much a necessity outside of the big cities, and memories are still fresh of the deprivations in the 1930's and the 'dust bowl' farmlands of the Mid West. Hard lessons were learnt during those years just before the 2nd World War. Of course, Americans take the notion of storing basics to extremes, at least by our standards. But you can't help admiring the enthusiastic way they approach the subject. If you have access to the Internet, try visiting a site such as www.backwoodshome.com for a few interesting recipes, and tips on assembling a store cupboard for a rainy day. Though I get the impression that their idea of a rainy day involves some sort of nuclear catastrophe!

In Britain our grandmother's generation had to put up with the deprivations of war-time rationing, which wasn't completely lifted until 1954. They quickly learnt about making-do and squirreling away things for their store cupboards, so their families didn't go hungry. An interesting fact about rationing is that although the weekly rations were impossibly tiny by today's standards, the general health of the nation improved because of the balanced diet that they were forced to eat.

These days we have freezers, and the infinitesimal possibilities of storing perishable foods for long periods of time. But it would be foolish to rely entirely on a freezer to tide you over emergencies, especially since the prospect of power cuts is apparently more and more of a possibility.

Firstly, a short lecture! The basis of an efficient store cupboard is organisation. And by that I mean decide which cupboard is going to be designated the store cupboard, and then write a list of all the basic ingredients you think you may need. Go through your existing supplies and throw out, or donate to a charity, all those strange tins and jars that have been lurking at the back of your cupboards and those three-quarter empty bags of undetermined flour. At the back of my cupboard I found an ancient can of Wichitty Grub soup, a very old present from a friend returning from Australia!

Once you have your list, rearrange the things you are going to keep in some sort of order, I'll leave the order up to you. Copy your list and stick it inside the cupboard door.

Divide the items you need to buy into 3 or 4 sections, and next time you go shopping, buy the most important items first, and then the next time the lesser important, and so on.

There is no point breaking the bank by trying to buy it all in one go.

How much of each item you buy and store is something you will have to decide. There is no point storing away hundreds of pounds worth of food. Try to think about what each item might be for, what the Americans call 'scenario planning'.

There is a useful maxim: 'Store what you Eat, and Eat What You Store'. The point of that is that you must use all the food in your cupboard, and replace it as you go. Think of it as a savings account for a rainy day. It must be used and not just hoarded. Rotation is the name of the game. Use the oldest items first and replace them promptly. ●

# Nelson's bread pudding

This my husband's Mum's recipe with an additional ingredient! Bread pudding is one of the oldest known puddings, with variations appearing down the centuries.

I discovered that in Norfolk this is sometimes known as Nelson's Cake after that famous son of Norfolk, Admiral Nelson. When our daughter was young we used to take her to Trafalgar Square to feed the pigeons with slices of stale bread. From her first visit she always said it was her Granddad on top of Nelson's Column! In a roundabout way this recipe reminds me of those happy days, and of course my days as an impoverished student. Bread pudding is not only the perfect store cupboard dish, it also keeps very well in the store cupboard. I've never yet met anyone who's eyes don'ít light up when offered a slice of bread pudding!

**225g (8oz) of stale bread, with the crusts, in feed-the-pigeons sized pieces!**
**175g (6oz) dried mixed fruit**
**1 tbsp marmalade**
**50g (2oz) dark brown sugar**
**2 tsp mixed spice**
**75g (3oz) butter, softened**
**1 egg, beaten**
**milk**
**small measure of dark rum, in homage to Nelson**

## METHOD

Soak the pieces of bread in a little milk for 45 minutes. Meanwhile soak the dried fruit in the rum, and stir in the marmalade. Then mix everything together, stirring until it is all mixed well and smooth. Grease an ovenproof dish, about 1.2 litre will do. Tip the mixture into the dish. Place in a preheated oven at 160ºC (325ºF, gas 3) for about 45 minutes, until the pudding has set. Serve hot or cold. I like custard with it!

# Sausage, apple and cider suet pudding

Steamed suet puddings are perennial favourites in my house! This is a very adaptable suet pudding, good enough to feed an entire family. All you need is 900g (2lb) of sausages, some bacon and a cup of cider, and your store cupboard. It takes minutes to prepare, but of course takes a while to steam and cook. So you can go off and do something else while it cooks!

Serves 4

**For the suet crust**
**450g (1lb) self raising flour**
**225g (8oz) shredded suet**
**1 tsp salt**
**1 tbspn chopped dried parsley**

**For the filling**
**900g (2lb) pork sausages, sliced and chopped, the best you can afford**
**225g (8oz) bacon, diced**
**1 tin of baked beans**
**1 large apple, grated (an old apple will do)**
**150ml (¼ pint) cider**
**1 onion sliced**
**Sage or thyme**

**METHOD**
Make the pastry crust by mixing all the pastry ingredients together with really cold water to make a firm dough. Roll the dough out onto a floured board. Grease a 1.2 litre pudding basin, and line with the rolled out dough, reserving enough for the lid.

Fill the pastry with alternate layers of the chopped sausage and the other ingredients. Finally add the cider and season with pepper and salt. All the ingredients shouldn't fill the basin completely. Wet the edge of the pastry liner and place the pastry lid in place, squeezing them together.

Cover loosely with a sheet of foil or greaseproof, and tie around with string. Wrap the whole bowl in a square of muslin, and tie a 'handle' on the top. Place the basin in a saucepan half-filled with simmering water and allow to steam for about two and a half hours. Keep an eye on the water level, and top up as necessary. Then remove the basin from the saucepan, carefully! Let the steaming hot bowl rest for about 15 minutes, then again carefully, remove the muslin and foil. Run a palette knife around the edges and turn out onto a serving dish. This goes very well with simply boiled and buttered potatoes and freshly ground black pepper.

# Sweetheart tart

'Treacle Tart' is rhyming slang for sweetheart, and down my way its not uncommon to hear people say, 'Alright treacle?', as if they've found themselves on the set of Eastenders! I rather like it as a term of endearment, much better than 'princess'. But this tart isn't too sweet, the lemon adds an edge to counteract the sweetness. My hubby doesn't like his tarts too sweet!

**225g (8oz) short crust pastry, ready made**
**2 tbsp black treacle**
**6-8 tbsp golden syrup**
**75g (3oz) fresh breadcrumbs**
**1 tbsp lemon juice and zest**
**Pinch ground cinnamon**

**METHOD**
Roll out the pastry. Using about two thirds of the pastry, line a loose ringed tin, a tin about 23cm-25cm (9 to 10 inches) in diameter. Put the remaining pastry to one side. Combine all the other ingredients, you may find it easier if you warm the syrups over a gentle heat and then add the other ingredients.

When everything is combined, pour into the pastry case. Return to the reserved pastry, rollout again and cut into strips. Using the strips of pastry, make a criss-cross lattice top to your tart, twisting the strips as you go. Push the ends of the strips into the rim of the case and then decorate the edge with a fork. Bake in a preheated oven at 190oC (375oF, gas 5) until the tart is golden. Serve warm or cold, not hot. I'd serve with cream or ice cream.

# Devilishly Delicious Halloween Treats

## *Forget the tricks, its time for Halloween treats*

**Clarissa Porter** offer
some treats to prepar
and make fo

## Devilled chicken

Supreme finger food! If you're having
stand-up party or maybe a bonfire, the
are great for a starter or main course.

Serves 4-6

**2 or 3 chicken drumsticks per perso**
**2 onions, sliced**
**2 carrots, sliced**
**2 sticks of celery, sliced**
**Bouquet Garni, parsley, bay, thyme**
**pepper and salt**

For the devilling sauce
**110g (3½oz) butter**
**2tbsp tomato ketchup**
**2tbsp Worcester sauce**
**2tbsp fruit chutney or mango chutne**
**Cayenne pepper**
**Ginger, small piece, grated**
**1 red chilli, chopped and seeded**
**pepper and salt**

### METHOD
Put the chicken drumsticks, onio
celery, carrots, and herbs into a pan a
just cover with water. Cook gently
about 15 minutes. Drain and co
Remove skin from the chicken when i
cool enough to handle. Whizz or pound
the other ingredients into a paste a
spread on the chicken. Grill or barbec
the drumsticks for about 6 minut
turning once.

become a time for dressing up and childrens' parties, the last day of October was the last day of the Celtic year. It was in fact New Year's Eve to e ancient Celts. The end of October meant trees sing their leaves, the end of grazing animals tdoors, choosing which of the livestock to ughter for food through the winter, the end of e harvest and the dying of the Sun. The coming mists and the shortening of days.

Hallowe'en was, in fact, the original Harvest stival. It was all about food, because food meant ng and surviving the long winter

A sacred bonfire would be lit on a prominent hill, last sacred fire of the year, following sacred fires lit he Spring and midsummer, and there would be emonial meals left as offerings to appease the rits.

It was also a time of the year when extended nilies came together to ready themselves for the dships of the Winter to come, and make stores of d that could be kept for use during the long cold nths ahead.

With the coming of Christianity in Europe, this gan festival became absorbed and adapted. The of November is All Saints Day in the Christian endar, conveniently allowing the 31st October to nain as All Hallow's (holy) Eve. Following the npowder Plot of 1605, and the subsequent ecution of Guy Fawkes and his pals, the 5th of vember became the time for the lighting of bonfires, d Hallowe'en as a festival went into decline.

However, the strict Protestant Scots who were igrating to North America at about this time took n them their traditions of the Harvest stival/Hallowe'en, and amalgamated it with the eat as they saw it, of Catholicism by the execution Guy Fawkes.

So, Halloween as a festival continued to be served, and flourished in North America.

In early Christian Britain, beggars would go from use to house offering to say prayers for the ceased in return for alms. The 'alms' became ritual s of small cakes, 'soul cakes'. This maybe the origin he much more recent practice of Trick or Treat, but one knows for sure. 'Trick or Treat' is first ntioned by name in a newspaper article from ifornia in the 1930's. Similarly, no-one knows the gins of the 'Jack O'Lantern' pumpkin head. The mpkin is a vegetable native to North America, ated to all the other squashes, and to cucumbers. It perfectly possible that the early settlers in North erica made lanterns from hollowed out pumpkins d turnips, but there is no descriptive evidence of ir history.

Maybe it has something to do with "Sleepy Hollow" d the legend of the headless horseman!

And so to today. As a child in the 1960's I knew of loween, but it wasn't an event celebrated in the y it is today. Infact, I don't remember it being ebrated at all.

It was when I first went to the USA in the mid '0's that I saw my first pumpkin heads on doorsteps Utah! And I went Trick or Treating with an American nily, then an unheard of custom in this country. But he last 20 years Hallowe'en has become a major nt once again in Britain, especially for children, ng over from Guy Fawkes night as a time when dren can enjoy themselves dressing up and go m house to house asking for 'Treats'. Strange how ory repeats itself! Many of you will be having ties at Hallowe'en, here are my ideas for party

# Devilled prawns

These make a lively starter, and can be eaten with your fingers indoors or out. A really quick and easy snack to get you Hallowe'en party off to a flying start!

Serves 4

**225g (7oz) raw prawns or shrimps, peeled with tail left on**
**110g (3½oz) butter**
**1 red chilli seeded and sliced**
**garlic, a few slivers**
**brandy, an optional splash**

## METHOD

Warm the butter in a large frying pan, and then toss in the prawns or shrimps. Add the garlic and chilli. When the prawns turn pink, serve them straight from the pan with some slices o good bread. If you want a spectacular finish to the dish, splash a little brandy in the pan at the last minute, and flame the prawns.

# Fiery gypsy stew

This is a lovely colourful dish that makes the most of a pumpkin or squash. The finishing thickening paste, or 'picada', can be adjusted to your personal taste. So as you mix the picada, keep tasting the mixture. The finished dish is fruity and sweet, so don't be put off by the thought of all that ginger and chilli! And this can be a spectacular dish if served in a hollowed-out pumpkin, or in individual hollowed-out squash!

Serves 8 or more

**450g (14oz) dried chickpeas, soaked overnight (or 3 tins of chickpeas)**

150ml (¼ pint) olive oil
2 onions, finely chopped
2 tomatoes, finely chopped
2 carrots, finely chopped
2 sticks of celery, finely chopped
450g (15oz) green beans, cut into 1 inch lengths
450g (15oz) pumpkin or other squash, peeled and cubed
2 firm pears, cubed
600ml (1 pint) vegetable stock (cube is fine)
salt and pepper

For the thickening 'picada'
2 slices of white bread, fried in olive oil
2 cloves of garlic
2tbsp ground almonds
3tbsp white wine vinegar
2tbsp paprika

pinch of saffron
1 or 2 red chillies, seeded and chopped
ginger, small piece grated

## METHOD

Either cook the pre-soaked chickpeas in plen of water for about 1 hour, or open 3 tins!

In a large pan, gently sweat the onion tomatoes, carrots and celery in the olive oil fo about 20 minutes till soft. Now add the stoc chickpeas, pumpkin and green beans an simmer gently for about 20 minutes. Add the chopped pears and cook for a further 1 minutes. Now, either whizz all the picac ingredients in a blender or, much more fu pound them with a pestle and mortar. The latte method is easier if you want to adjust the flavou Now stir the picada into the stew to thicken Serve.

# Spicy fruits in a paper bag

the chocolate cake was too grown-up for the youngsters, these paper parcels will be just the ticket! You can vary the uit ingredients and use whatever you have handy. Dried uit can be used mixed in with the fresh fruit, and for grown-o parcels you can soak the dried fruit in brandy or tea. ither way this is a delightfully messy and surprising udding, and warming too for your little Hallowe'eners.

ervers 4

sheets of greaseproof paper about 12 inches square, use sheets per parcel, laid on top of each other.
**punnet of raspberries**
**pears, sliced**
**apricots, halved**
**banana, sliced**

**dried figs, soaked in tea or brandy**
**bananas, sliced**
**pears, sliced**

whatever combination suits your taste

**ice of 2 oranges, and their zest**
**pieces of cinnamon stick**
**little grated nutmeg**
**few mixed peppercorns**
**knob of butter per serving**
**tbsp brown sugar or maple syrup**

## ETHOD

reheat your oven to 200ºC (400ºF, gas 6). Divide the fruit etween the 4 paper squares, keeping the fruit towards the iddle. Add the orange juice and zest, spices, sugar, and utter. Now fold up the paper squares, either twist at the top and tie with string to secure, or pleat the aper across the top and twist the ends like a cracker. Put a little boiling water in a roasting tray, place e parcels gently on top of the water and put them in the oven for 6 to 7minutes. Carry to the table, urst the parcels and serve with vanilla ice cream.

# Devilishly naughty chocolate cake

No, this isn't spicy, but it is certainly naughty! Very easy to make, I've scrumped this recipe from my friend Terri, she uses butter icing, but I've made a chocolate 'ganache'. If you double up on the ingredients, it will fill a roasting tin, very good for parties! And one for the grown-ups!

**175g (6oz) self raising flour**
**110g (3½oz) sugar**
**4tbsp of good cocoa powder**
**1tsp baking powder**
**1 dessert spoon of treacle or**
**golden syrup 150mls sunflower oil**
**150 mls milk**
**2 eggs**

## METHOD
Put all the ingredients into a blender and whizz together.

Pour into a greased cake tin. Cover with buttered paper and cook in a medium oven for about 1hour

Test with a skewer and cook for a few more minutes if necessary allow to cool and turn out onto a plate

Now you have to make the 'ganache', which is a sort of saucyicing, or icing sauce.

You will need
**250g very good plain**
**chocolate125ml cream**
**3.5 tbs. creme fraiche**
**65g butter**

To make the 'ganache'
Melt the chocolate in a large bowl placed over a saucepan of boiling water gradually combine the creams and butter until the mixture is smooth.

Go back to the cake, slice the cake into squares and pile up in a heap, now pour over the chocolate sauce and serve with cream.

# One Pot Wonders

There is something very comforting about one pot meals, perhaps they are evocative of childhood, or maybe some kind of long-forgotten memory, says **Clarissa Porter**

## Chicken with garlic and fennel

Serves 4

85g (3oz) butter
3 bulbs of fennel sliced lengthways
2 carrots roughly chopped
1 bulb of garlic, separated
1 medium chicken, jointed into 4 or 8 pieces
Quarter of a bottle of dry white wine
1 tbsp of French mustard
Bunch of fresh thyme
500ml (1 pint) of chicken stock
A little plain flour

**METHOD**

Place a large flameproof oven dish on the stove, melt half the butter and add the chopped, sliced vegetables. Move the vegetables around for a minute or two.

Remove from the heat and lay the chicken pieces on top of the vegetables. Combine the mustard, wine, and stock, and pour over the chicken. Scatter some sprigs of thyme over the dish. Place in an oven heated to 180°C (350°F, gas 4) for about an hour. Remove and strain the liquid into a saucepan, then mash the butter into the flour to make a paste, whisk this slowly into the liquid to make a sauce. Pour over the chicken and serve.

It doesn't take a genius to realise that the origin of these dishes is very ancient indeed, from the time when it was usual to cook over an open fire. Every country in the world has its own history of dishes, held in their national memory.

Our tradition is linked with that of our European neighbours. Without going too far back into the mists of time, we can trace our present day one pot dishes back nearly 2,000 years to when Roman soldiers in Britain existed on 'pottage'.

Pottage was a dish of many ingredients: hunks of meat, oatmeal, vegetables, herbs and even fish! From this came 'porridge', and later the word 'porray', which in turn became 'purée'. Gradually over the next 1,000 years this dish evolved, with rich people eating more refined versions, and the poor making-do with whatever they could get.

By the time of Elizabeth I peas and lentils with bacon in a stock thickened with cornflour was the staple dish of most of the poor people in the countryside. Peas and beans would be dried and stored, and most people kept a pig. Pottage with dried peas could be made into a pudding, and this is where we get Pease Pudding, an old-fashioned recipe that I can remember from my childhood. Pottage made with dried beans is the ancestor of today's baked beans. So next time you open a tin of baked beans, take time to reflect that you are continuing a tradition, a direct link with the diet of the Middle Ages!

By the Nineteenth Century pottage had been renamed 'stew'. I don't know about you, but does anyone have any happy memories of 'stews'? We took the word 'stew' from the French 'estuver', but the French have kept the word 'potage' which now means soup. They also have the wonderful phrase the 'Pot Au Feu', literally, the pot at the fire, or more accurately, the stock pot. But did you know that when applied to a person it can also mean 'someone who stays at home'? How did we end up with 'stew'?

One thing is certain, although these one pot recipes have evolved and achieved a certain sophistication, they are good honest dishes, from a long tradition firmly rooted in the countryside of this island. I suggest you serve them with crusty bread and a simple green salad.

Country Cooking

# Guinea fowl with red cabbage

Serves 4

**1 large Guinea fowl**
**6 shallots, chopped**
**55g (2oz) butter**
**1 medium red cabbage, chopped into strips**
**2 apples, skin on, cored and chopped**
**85g (3oz) sultanas**
**170g (6oz) streaky bacon**
**Large glass white wine**
**Freshly ground black pepper**
**2 tbsp of sherry vinegar**
**A little honey**

**METHOD**

Using a heavy cast iron pan, big enough to hold all the ingredients, fry the chopped shallots in a little butter.

Place the Guinea fowl in the pan on the hob, and brown on all sides, turning the fowl. Lift out the Guinea fowl and de-glaze the pan with the wine.

Put the slices of red cabbage and all the remaining ingredients, except the sherry vinegar, into the pan. Nestle the guinea fowl among the cabbage.

Cover loosely with foil, and cook in a moderate oven and forget it for about 90 minutes! Then remove from the oven, drizzle the vinegar over the dish and adjust the seasoning to taste.

# One pot bacon with baby vegetables

1 joint of collar of bacon
1 small green cabbage
280g (10 oz) of each of the following: baby leeks, baby carrots, baby turnips, small new potatoes
1 onion with one clove
1 bay leaf
Bunch of curly leafed parsley
Any boiling sausage, about 255g (9-10oz) chopped into large chunks
A few black peppercorns

**METHOD**

Soak the bacon joint overnight in cold water. Cut the cabbage into large slices. Arrange the bacon, cabbage, sausage, bay leaf, peppercorns and parsley in a large casserole dish, or a jam saucepan will do nicely. Cover with water, and gently simmer for about an hour. Add the new potatoes, and 10 minutes later add the rest of the baby vegetables.

Simmer until vegetables are tender. Serve with pickles and mustard and crusty bread... and masses of finely chopped parsley.

# English country pork and beans

This is an adaptation of an old English farm workers' dish, easy to make and virtually indestructible. Definitely better the next day, and even better the day after that!

**900g (2lb) shoulder or leg of pork, diced**
**170g (6oz) streaky bacon, chopped**
**2-3 onions, sliced**
**2-3 sticks of celery, sliced**
**2-3 carrots sliced**
**225g (8oz) butter beans, soaked overnight**
**400g (14oz) tin of tomatoes**
**2 tbsp of tomato purée**
**85g (3oz) lard or dripping**
**2 tsp English mustard**
**1 clove of garlic**
**Bunch of fresh thyme**
**2 tbsp of honey or maple syrup**
**Salt & pepper**

### METHOD

Melt the lard in a deep heavy pan, large enough to take everything. Add the bacon pieces, onion, celery, carrots, and garlic and allow to soften. Remove from the heat and add the beans, diced pork, tomatoes and puree and season to taste.

Cover with boiling water. Either cover pan with lid or foil, and place in oven heated to 170°C (340°F, gas 3-4) and leave for about 2½ to 3 hours.

The beans will then be creamy, and the meat very tender. This will feed lots of hungry people!

# Time to start smoking!

**Clarissa Porter** loves smoked fish and here she shares some of her favourite recipes with us

Fish have been preserved by smoking since prehistoric times. Smoking was the preferred method to store fish to eat during the long winter months. Another strange method of preserving food, including fish, was by burying it in the cold earth. Our ancestors would have been very familiar with 'smoked salmon', since the salmon was one of the most plentiful fish in our rivers. In the Middle Ages, smoked salmon was on sale in the streets of London, and the River Thames teemed with salmon right up to the dawn of the Industrial Revolution. Salmon, along with lobsters and oysters, had an unenviable reputation as food for the masses. The upper classes wouldn't countenance eating salmon lest they were assumed to have fallen on hard times. But, by the mid 19th century, salmon had all but disappeared from the Thames. Pollution had driven them away. Salmon need clean fresh water to spawn, and so suddenly they were in short supply, the price rocketed, and the upper classes took to dining on salmon.

Salmon may have disappeared from the Thames, but it was still being caught elsewhere in the country, but not in any great numbers. Writing in 1907, the great French chef Escoffier praised the salmon from the River Severn, saying it was amongst the finest in Europe.

Nowadays, with modern fish farming methods, Salmon is ubiquitous and cheap. Most of the salmon on sale in supermarkets, fresh or smoked, will be farmed, but it is not difficult to buy wild salmon. Of course I believe wild salmon to be superior to the farmed salmon, and most, if not all, of the smoked salmon you see on sale in supermarkets will be farmed and mass produced in huge kilns. Unfortunately a large proportion of the industrially produced smoked salmon will have been dyed to produce that deep orange tone.

There are two basic methods of smoking fish:

Cold Smoking, and Hot Smoking, in the following descriptions of the methods I am describing traditional methods, not the large-scale industrial operations.

Cold Smoking is the older and therefore more original method. It is also the more difficult method for an inexperienced smoker. The Smoke House is traditionally a small wooden building, sometimes

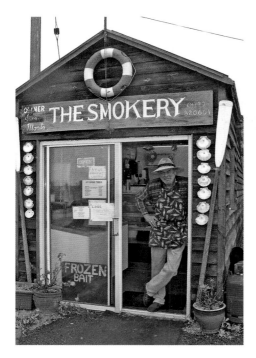

called The Hang, which derives from Herring Hang. The fish are hung from racks above a ring of smouldering oak sawdust. How high above the sawdust depends on the size and type of fish. Salmon would normally be at the highest point, maybe 6 feet above the sawdust. This method is called Cold Smoking because the fish are cooked by the smoke, little or no heat is involved. If you were to reach into the smoke house during the process and touch the fish, it would feel cold. How long they hang in the smoke house depends on many things, but salmon can take as long as five days to cure, because oily fish take longer to absorb the smoke. And you can't rush a good thing. The time of the year plays its part in timing the length of a smoke, outside temperature is important, and high humidity can ruin a smoke, colder winter temperatures are better. Salmon cured this way are ready to be eaten without any other preparation. Other fish, such as haddock or herring would need to be cooked after cold smoking.

Hot Smoking is done in a much smaller container, something like a kiln, usually made of stainless steel these days. The fish are laid on racks in layers. At the bottom of the smoker is a hot plate, sawdust is spread on this plate, and the plate is heated from beneath by gas or electricity. This causes the sawdust to spark and smoulder. The fish are then cooked by a combination of smoke and heat, and need no further cooking, apart from maybe re heating before serving.

Oak sawdust is the preferred type, but some would say that the dust from fruit trees is as good, or maybe a combination of fruit and oak sawdust.

But, I have left out a very important part of the process. Before the fish is smoked, it must be thoroughly salted. This removes excess water from the fish, and imparts flavour. Water in the fish

carries bacteria, so this is an important part of the process, and a pleasant result of the salting is that the smoked fish develops a glaze, which enhances the appearance of the finished product.

The fish are normally left for three or four hours in the salt flakes, salmon take a little longer than some fish because they are oily fish. Oak smoke also has antiseptic properties, the more smoke and the more salt, the longer the fish will keep. The salt is rinsed off before the smoking begins.

You can try hot smoking at home, using a large kettle barbecue. First, salt your fish, I used salmon fillets, for at least three hours, then rinse and dry on some kitchen tissue. Place a layer of charcoal in the barbecue, light and allow to burn until it is almost extinguished. Then sprinkle a layer of oak sawdust onto the embers. Place the fish on the grill. Replace the lid, leaving the ventilator very slightly open. And wait, try to resist lifting the lid for at least two hours, but if you think the sawdust has gone out or is exhausted add more sawdust and re-light. Then have a look, you should be able to gauge by look and maybe a prod or two whether the fish is cooked or needs longer, salmon should never be over cooked.

I have heard you can hot smoke in a wok (with a lid) indoors on a hob, but it is probably best if you have a smoke extractor. Using a wok would be ideal for experimenting with other smoking materials, such as tea leaves. Some of the more exotic scented teas mixed with sawdust should produce interesting flavours. If you like the idea of hot smoking your own fish, you can buy a proper hot smoker from suppliers such as Cookequip (www.cookequip.co.uk ).

My research for this article took me to Dungeness, actually I don't need much of an excuse to visit The Ness, because my favourite smokery is there. If you've never been there, Dungeness is a strange, bleak, and wild place, officially a desert, the only desert in the UK. The largest expanse of shingle in Europe, and second only to Cape Canaveral in the World. Spread out along the only road are the old shacks of the fishing community. Winter is ideal for an atmospheric visit, cold and windswept, and offering a glimpse of the hardships the inhabitants must have suffered before the coming of electricity, bottled gas, and central heating oil! The day I visited the rain was lashing down. As I struggled across the shingle dragging my poor reluctant lurcher along behind me, I was surprised and

pleased to see a small group of fishermen with rods trying to cast into the crashing waves. I stood for a few moments watching the fishermen, and listening to the strange electronic fog signal coming from the nearby lighthouse, then the soaking lurcher nudged me and reminded me why we had come here.

Jim Moate lives in Pearl Cottage, which dates back 270 years. Next door is his Smokery. Jim has been smoking fish here for 30 years, but there has been a smokery in use at Pearl Cottage for over 200 years. (The Smokery, Dungeness, opens Tuesday to Sunday. Tel: 01797 320604)

Jim told me that he'd found an old price list scrawled on newspapers used as wallpaper, Bloaters - 18d per hundred.

Bloaters are smoked herrings, like kippers but smoked whole. The original red herring. They were the most popular smoked fish 100 years ago, and just about unobtainable now, unless you know of a very traditional fishmonger or smokery. Jim started as a fisherman living and working at Dungeness, but an injury ended his fishing career.

Years ago, every house at Dungeness would have had its own smokery, and after his injury stopped him going back to sea, Jim Moate asked the older fishermen for their recipes. With practice, Jim developed his own skills and methods.

If you find yourself nearby, I recommend a trip to Dungeness and The Smokery. Jim Moate is an amiable and approachable expert, enthusiastically talking about his craft, and sharing his experience. It was Jim that encouraged me to try smoking my own fish using a BBQ.

Buying direct from a small smokery like Jim's should ensure you are getting the best of everything, no dyes, chemicals or preservatives are used here. Jim also uses his skills to smoke cheese and garlic, but he has had to stop smoking meat too many regulations. As I drove home from The Ness, darkness falling fast and the car filled with the smell of smoked fish and damp lurcher, I found myself plotting when I could find the time to escape back there.

And so to the recipes, the most important thing to remember about serving smoked salmon is to keep the dish as simple as possible, the flavour of the smoked fish is robust, and there is no point introducing a clash of flavours. Escoffier said that however Salmon is prepared, it should be served plainly, and always with (his) cucumber salad. •

# Home-made hot smoked salmon

Inspired by Jim Moate, I hot smoked my salmon fillets on a barbecue using oak sawdust I managed to get from my local timber merchant, mixed with some chippings from a neighbour's apple trees. There was a bit of trial and error. But they tasted delicious. Of course it is time consuming, so it is probably more practical to buy them ready smoked. But I wanted to try it at least once. After they had cooled (I smoked them the day before) I heated the fillets in parcels before serving.

**1 salmon fillet per person**
**new potatoes**
**broccoli**
**3 eggs**
**2 lemons**
**salt and pepper**
**butter**

**METHOD**

Place each fillet on a square of greaseproof paper, and dot with butter and a little pepper. Twist the paper into a cracker shape. Put into an oven at 180ºC (350ºF, gas 4) for about 15 to 20 minutes.

Meanwhile steam the broccoli, I'll leave the amounts up to you, but don't overcook, the broccoli should be firm not squashy. While this is happening you can be boiling the new potatoes, and making the lemon sauce. To make the sauce, whisk the eggs and the juice of the 2 lemons into a bowl balanced over a saucepan of lightly boiling water. Whisk till mixture is frothy, then add a little salt to taste.

Serve the salmon still in the parcels, with a few potatoes on the side, and the broccoli, and the lemon sauce drizzled over the vegetables.

# Home cured salmon with tarragon

This dish is as old as smoked salmon, and easier to make at home. The origins of this method of preserving are lost in the mists of time, but it harks back to when our ancestors buried food as a way of preserving it! The Swedes call this 'Gravad Lax', from the Swedish gravad meaning buried, and lax which is Swedish for salmon. It is one of my personal favourite dishes, I was introduced to it at the start of my career in food, when for a while I was helping Keith Floyd on photo sessions. He introduced this dish to me at his home in Devon. Once made, this dish will keep for at least a week, but you can't freeze it. It usually tastes best three or four days after preparation.

Traditionally this is made with dill, but I have made this variation with tarragon out of deference to a friend of mine who has an aversion to dill.

**1-1.5kg (2lb-2lb 5oz) fresh whole salmon, gutted, fillet, head removed, skin on**
**Handful (large handful) of fresh tarragon, chopped**
**4tbsps coarse sea salt**
**2tbsps sugar**
**2tbsps black peppercorns**

Tarragon mustard sauce
**2tbsp whole grain mustard**
**1 egg yolk**
**1tbsp sugar**
**2tbsp white wine vinegar**
**150ml oil (sunflower or groundnut)**
**2tbsp tarragon, chopped**
**rock salt**
**ground black pepper**
**lemon wedges**

## METHOD

You need two same size pieces of salmon, so after removing head and tail and filleting to remove bones, cut the fish into two lengthways. So you have two similar sized pieces.

You will need a suitable dish on which to lay the fillets, but it must not be aluminium, plastic would be ideal. Lay one of the fillets, skin down, on the dish. Crush the peppercorns roughly, and then mix together the peppercorns, tarragon, sea salt, and sugar. Sprinkle this mixture across the salmon, generously. Now place the other fillet, skin up, on top making a sandwich. Place a piece of greaseproof paper or cling film over the fish, and then place a board or plate (a piece of hardboard would do) on top of the fish. Place some weights on top of the board, a few tins will do, and place in the fridge for at least 48 hours, but preferably 72 hours. Every 12 hours or so, turn the fish over. The juices will be running out of the fish, and every time you turn it, spoon the juices over the fish, like basting a piece of meat.

Before you serve the salmon, make a sauce of mustard and tarragon: mix together the egg yolk, mustard and sugar together in a bowl. Then gradually stir in the oil with a whisk.

Stir in the vinegar and chopped Tarragon, then season with salt and pepper to your taste.

To serve the salmon, slice it at an angle so that you get thickish slices. Arrange on your plate and serve with the sauce, and maybe some interesting bread.

# Smoked salmon and cucumber salad

This is the classic smoked salmon dish, as recorded by Escoffier in 1907. The salmon has been cold smoked by the classic method, and you can either buy it ready sliced in paper-thin slices, or I personally prefer to buy a side of salmon, which would weigh about 500g (1lb 2oz), and slice it myself. Because I prefer thicker slices! Please just lay it flat on the plate, don't try arty curls of salmon. The deep pink of the fish is perfectly set off by the cucumber salad, but if you prefer you could use any green leaves, preferably roughly chopped, as an accompaniment.

**100g-175g (4oz-6oz) of cold smoked salmon per person**
**2 cucumbers, peeled**
**small bunch of chervil**
**salt and pepper**
**vinegar**

## METHOD

To make the cucumber salad, take your two peeled cucumbers, cut them into two along their length, and remove the seeds. Then mince them with a grater or very finely chop them. Put the minced cucumber in to a bowl and sprinkle with ordinary table salt. This will draw out moisture from the cucumber. Leave for about half an hour, then drain and place the cucumbers on a clean fluff free tea towel, fold over and press. Scrape into a small bowl and season with pepper, a little olive oil and vinegar to taste.

Then add some chopped chervil.

Serve the salmon simply on the plate with a little pile of cucumber salad, and some brown bread.

Winter

# Not such small fry

Serve up these tasty
morsels and you won't need
to fish for compliments, says
**_Clarissa Porter_**

## Lord Mayor's sprats

This is an old English dish and makes a splendid light lunch. November 9th was Lord Mayor's Day in London, and it coincided with the arrival in London of smoked Suffolk sprats. The unfortunate Lord Mayors found their day teasingly renamed 'Sprat Day'!

**2 or 3 smoked sprats per person**
**Dry white wine**
**Brown bread and butter**
**Ground black pepper**

**METHOD**
Skin and fillet each sprat (this is easily done) or leave whole, as I have, if you much prefer. Pile attractively on a serving dish and pour over a little dry white wine. Place in a refrigerator and chill thoroughly. Serve with brown bread and butter, and some more white wine to toast the Lord Mayor.

Some 150 years ago, riverside inns along the banks of the Thames would have thronged with people eating whitebait. They were caught in the Thames estuary in huge numbers. The Trafalgar Inn at Greenwich was the venue for an annual whitebait supper, held by the government, usually the Liberals; the Conservatives held theirs in the now demolished Ship Inn near by. If you find yourself in Greenwich, seek out the Trafalgar. I can't guarantee they'll have whitebait on the menu but the riverside views and the ambience will make up it.

Whitebait are the young of herring, very economical and readily available – although you'll probably have to buy them frozen, especially around winter time.

Sprats can be found fresh, or you can buy them frozen. Like whitebait they were once fished in the lower Thames, now they are caught further out in the estuary off Southend. Both are rich in Omega 3, with its associated health benefits.

Sprats look like small herring and are quite often sold smoked or cured. November is good time to look for sprats and dabs in your local fishmongers. Dabs are small flat fish, similar to flounder but much tastier, and must be eaten really fresh. Unfortunately, they have fallen out of fashion and it may take a trip to the coast to find a fishmonger stocking them.

Sardines are readily available, probably imported, quite possibly caught off our coasts by foreign boats, and then exported back to us!

These are the four fish I've chosen for my recipes. Fry is the word for young fish but, while small fry is a somewhat derogatory term, implying insignificance, there's nothing uninspiring about these dishes! They are tasty and good for you, and fish is still, mostly, a wild food. It is also surprisingly easy to cook and remarkably quick. What are you waiting for? ●

"Fry is the word for young fish but, while small fry is a somewhat derogatory term... there's nothing uninspiring about these dishes!"

# Kentish devilled whitebait

There is really only one way to cook whitebait and that is to fry them. If you cook them using the method below, you'll find you've created the devil of a dish!

Serves 4

**450g (14oz) whitebait (don't clean them, you eat them whole)**
**100g (4oz) flour**
**250ml (8fl oz) milk**
**1tsp salt**
**1tsp cayenne pepper, plus a little more for dusting**
**Half or quarter of lemon**
**Bunch of parsley**
**Vegetable oil for frying**

**METHOD**
Place the whitebait in a large bowl with the milk for 4 to 5 minutes. Remove and drain. Mix your flour with salt and Cayenne pepper. Put the flour mixture in a plastic bag, add the whitebait, and shake gently to coat the fish lightly in the flour. Heat the vegetable oil to 180-190°C (375°F). A deep fat frier is the safest method, but you could use a deep saucepan. Shake off the excess flour from the fish. Divide into four portions and fry each portion separately for no longer than two minutes. (If you fry them all together they may stick together). Drain them on kitchen paper and keep warm in the oven. When they are all cooked, serve with a piece of lemon, brown bread and butter and, lastly, sprinkle a little cayenne over the fish.

# Sardine salad sandwich

This is a bit of a family joke in our house. A couple of years ago we looked after a friend's two teenage children and, if there were any altercations, I would threaten the instigator, usually Lee, with a sardine salad in the bath (he hated sardines and baths). He would probably enjoy this recipe now that he has grown up and his tastes have expanded beyond pizza and chips!

Serves 4

**1-3 sardines per person, boned and filleted (you can buy sardines already prepared this way)**
**A little flour, pepper and salt**
**Oil for shallow frying**
**Chilli, 1 or 2 red and green, de-seeded**
**Garlic, 1 or 2 cloves**
**Lemon or lime juice from 1 fruit**
**Small bunches of parsley, coriander**
**Olive oil**
**Salad leaves**
**Cucumber, sliced**
**Pitta bread**

### METHOD

Make a paste by combining the chilli, garlic, lemon juice, parsley and coriander, olive oil (about two tablespoons), pepper and salt in a pestle and pound together.

Coat the sardines in the paste and chill for about 30 minutes. Then dust the sardines in a little flour, seasoned with pepper and salt. Coat them one at a time, they are fragile.

Shallow fry each side for about one minute. Drain and place into pitta bread, previously warmed, or use really good bread, and serve with salad leaves and cucumber.

Who wouldn't want this sardine salad in the bath?

# Dabs grilled with lemon butter

I love Dabs. They must be very fresh. Whenever I visit my favourite fish merchant in Cockle Shed Row, Leigh on Sea, I buy loads and we eat them as soon as I get home.

**1 or 2 dabs per person (ask the fishmonger to clean them for you)**
**15g (?oz) of butter per dab**
**Half a lemon with zest per dab**
**Salt and pepper**
**English (curly) parsley, washed and dried**
**Vegetable oil for deep frying**

### METHOD

Mash the lemon zest (and juice) into the butter with some pepper and a little salt, and chill. Turn your grill on to a high heat. Put a little of your chilled lemon butter onto each fish and grill, turn once and add more butter. No more than three minutes per side.

While you are grilling the fish, heat the oil in a deep-fat fryer. When it has reached the correct temperature, drop in a whole sprig of parsley and fry till it is crisp. The parsley must be completely dry before it goes into the hot oil.

Serve the dabs simply with another piece of lemon as a garnish, plus the fried parsley and with some good bread.

# WHIZZ-BANG FOOD!

***Clarissa Porter*** dreams up some delicious dishes that will recall Bonfire Night celebrations of yesteryear

2006 marked the 400th anniversary of the first 5th November celebration. In 1605 Guy Fawkes and his band of luckless co-conspirators failed to blow-up the Houses of Parliament and a year later the first bonfires were lit on the anniversary, and effigies burnt.

This was not just a spontaneous celebration, it was decreed that this should happen and, apparently, until 1959 it was illegal not to celebrate Guy Fawkes' arrest! So let's do it!

Bring friends and family together to enjoy a 400-year-old tradition amid the smell of gunpowder, wood smoke and food mingling together on a chill, crisp and, hopefully, dry evening.

When I was young, Bonfire Night was anticipated and planned for long in advance. Once the summer holidays were over it was the next exciting event to look forward to. Beginning in September, I would save my pocket money to buy fireworks. When they went on sale I would be first in the queue, spending my savings! In the weeks leading up to the night, I would buy more, one a week – I didn't get much pocket money! Most evenings I'd take my fireworks out of their box and line them up and count them, anticipating the thrill of seeing the colours, hearing the bangs, whizzes and whooshes of rockets and Catherine wheels, and remembering that unique smell.

The grown-ups were more concerned with the party and the food, leaving the fireworks to the children. How times have changed. But memories of those childhood Bonfire Nights have stayed with me. I remember the evenings when it never stopped raining, when brief dashes were made into the garden to light fireworks, followed by a quick retreat back indoors to watch the explosions in the warm and the dry. I remember the night when the best laid plans

went wrong, and the box of fireworks exploded unintentionally and haphazardly. Mostly I remember the nights when all of our family seemed to come together and, with a few close friends, enjoy the sort of family party that somehow never happened at any other time of the year. Indoors and outdoors, wrapped up against the cold with damp woolly gloves, holding a sparkler in one hand and a sausage in the other!

Theses days, at least in towns and cities, I suspect most people go to organised firework displays, and the only food available is probably the hot-dog van parked in some boggy corner. The cost of fireworks has rocketed and in these risk-averse times it seems the easiest option.

But, if you are lucky enough to live in Sussex, near to the South Downs, several villages have Bonfire Societies, and hold very traditional celebrations, making their own fireworks and burning huge bonfires, with sometimes topical and controversial Guys. The biggest of these celebrations is held in Lewes, where some 50,000 people attend a night to remember.

But, if you want your Bonfire Night to be something your children will remember, you have to reclaim the night and hold your own celebration. Get together with your family and spread the cost of the fireworks, or invite everybody to bring a small selection box of fireworks.

## The food doesn't have to be expensive to be special.

Some of it can be prepared beforehand and warmed-up later or eaten cold, and some can be cooked in the bonfire itself. This time of the year would be a splendid excuse to cook some traditional 17th century food, for instance mutton pies would have been eaten at the time of the Gunpowder Plot, and anything with apples or

pears would also have been usual then.

Apple 'puffes', a sort of apple omelette, would have been familiar to Guy Fawkes, and almost any meat mixed with dried fruit and baked in a pie, which in those days was called a'coffyne'. In fact, the diet of the landed classes was exotic by today's tastes, including lark, sparrow, blackbird, sheep's tongue, umble pie (umble is the entrails of deer) – enhanced by most of today's herbs and spices, with the emphasis on nutmeg, mace, parsley and oregano. They also enjoyed all sorts of fish and shellfish, particularly oysters, venison, rabbit, hare... the list goes on and on.

Recipe books were being published, and dishes from Italy and France were commonplace in the great houses of town and country. In 1615, the young, future King Charles is recorded as breakfasting on chicken, beef, bread and beer. Although, apparently, he wasn't keen on beer, preferring orange juice!

Here are my suggestions for your party food, traditional like the event itself, yet sufficiently unusual to be remembered in years to come.

# Toffee apples

Apples are plentiful at this time of the year. In Guy Fawkes' time toffee apples were made with honey and beeswax, because sugar from the West Indies was expensive.

Makes 8

**8 eating apples**
**8 wooden sticks**
**225g (7oz) brown sugar**
**25g (1oz) butter**
**1 tbsp golden syrup**
**5 tbsp water**
**1 tsp vinegar**

**METHOD**

Wash and dry the apples well, and push in the sticks. Place the toffee ingredients in a heavy pan and heat gently till the sugar dissolves. Bring to the boil, that should be at about 140°C. You can test this by dipping a fork in the toffee and dripping a drop in a saucer of cold water. It should set and snap. Dip the apples in the hot toffee, twist to coat, remove and plunge into a bowl of cold water to set. Stand them on a tray to dry. When they have set hard, they can be wrapped in cellophane to keep.

"When I was young, Bonfire Night was anticipated and planned for long in advance."

# Mutton pies

If you can't get mutton, use lamb. One large pie would have been traditional but I've chosen to make individual pies, which can be easily held in the hand around your bonfire.
Make them in advance, and warm them up at the last minute.

**1 packet of short crust pastry, ready made**
**A little flour for rolling out**
**A little butter to grease the tins**
**225g (7oz) mutton, diced small**
**1 medium onion, diced small**
**1 small swede, diced small**
**1 carrot, diced small**
**½ tsp each of cinnamon, nutmeg, and mace**
**Large raisins, 6 per pie**
**Pepper and salt**
**Water or stock**
**1 egg, beaten**

## METHOD
You will need two muffin mould tins to make about 12 pies. Put everything, except the pastry, egg and flour, into a bowl and mix thoroughly. Roll out the pastry on a floured board. Line the muffin moulds, reserving some pastry for the lids. Place a large spoonful of the mixture into each mould. Cut out lids for each mould from the remaining pastry. Seal and glaze with the beaten egg. Make a small hole in the centre of each pie with a skewer. Place in an oven heated to 190°C (375°F, gas 5) for about 30 minutes until they are golden. The smell and appearance should guide you to the correct time! I would serve with cider.

# Yorkshire pudding trenchers

A trencher was a 'plate', made of wood or bread, onto which was served the meat for your meal. If it was made of bread, the juices from the meal soaked into the bread and you could eat the trencher as well! You can use these Yorkshire pudding trenchers instead of burger buns to hold your sausages, and give your guests something to talk about.

Makes 6 puddings

**125g (4oz) plain flour**
**½ tsp salt**
**1 large egg**
**300ml (½ pint) milk**
**2 tbsp cold water**
**Dripping, or a little butter**

## METHOD
You will need some muffin tins, or individual small pie tins, about 10cm (4ins) in diameter – how many depends on the number of guests at your bonfire party.

Sieve the flour into a bowl, add the salt, mix in the egg, then beat in the milk and water until you have a smooth batter. Cover with a tea towel and leave for one hour.

Either put a little dripping into each pie mould, or butter and maybe a hint of Marmite. Place the tins into a very hot oven till the dripping or butter is very hot, then put some of the batter into each tin – two or three tablespoons should do. Put back into the oven for about 15 minutes at 200°C (400°F, gas 6), until they have risen.

Remove and serve warm, if possible, on a white napkin with your sausages and horseradish.

> "Mostly I remember the nights when all of our family seemed to come together and, with a few close friends, enjoy the sort of family party that somehow never happened at any other time of the year."

# Very sticky ginger gake

This is my version of a very old recipe. Gingerbread was well known at the time of the Gunpowder Plot, even commemorated in a children's' rhyme that has come down the years, which ends: "when he's dead boil his head, make him into gingerbread".

100g (4oz) butter
100g (4oz) dark brown sugar
175g (6oz) black treacle
175g (6oz) golden syrup
90ml (3fl oz) warm milk

**4 pinches each of ground ginger, cinnamon, nutmeg**
**6-8 pieces of preserved stem ginger, roughly chopped**
**A little of the syrup the stem ginger was preserved in**
**50ml (1¼ fl oz) ginger wine**
**1 tsp cream of tartar**
**350g (11oz) plain flour**
**3 eggs, beaten**
**Juice and zest of 1 orange**

## METHOD

Mix together butter and sugar till fluffy and pale. Add the treacle, syrup, milk, spices, ginger wine, stem ginger and a little of the stem ginger syrup. Beat well together with a wooden spoon. Add the beaten eggs, mix in, then fold in the sifted flour and cream of tartar. Now add the orange juice and zest and fold again. Pour the mixture into a very well greased or lined baking tin, about 30cm (12in) by 22cm (8? in). Place in a pre-heated oven at 180°C (350°F, gas 4) for 45 to 60 minutes. Cool on a wire rack. Serve.

# Fiery bonfire potatoes

Potatoes would have been a recent addition to early 17th century meals!

**1 large potato per person, washed and dried**
**Cumin seeds**
**Salt**
**Olive or vegetable oil**

**METHOD**
Roll the dry potato in some oil, then in cumin seeds and salt. Wrap in foil and either bake in the embers of the bonfire, or bake in an oven, 200°C (400F, gas 6) for about an hour. Serve hot with butter. These will keep your hands warm.

# Marmalade sawceges (sausages)

Sausages are ideal at a bonfire party – children can eat them and warm their hands at the same time! Your butcher may have to order the skins for you. Use marmalade and pork or, better still and more authentic, game.

**900g (1lb 13oz) of belly of pork, or a half-and-half mixture of pork and game (like venison), very finely minced.**
**350g (11oz) shredded beef suet**
**225g (7oz) fresh white bread crumbs**
**1 heaped tbsp of best quality rough cut marmalade**
**½ tsp each of nutmeg, sage and thyme**
**Pepper and salt**
**Dash of whisky**
**Sausage skin**

**METHOD**
Mix all the ingredients together and fill a forcing bag (icing bag). Using a wide nozzle, force the mixture into the skin, twisting off sausage lengths as you go. Children often love to help with this part. Cut into sausages, prick the skins with a fork and fry or grill the usual way. Serve on trenchers made of Yorkshire Pudding with a little horseradish cream.

# Horseradish cream

Horseradish used to be used for medicinal purposes. It was supposed to aid digestion. I remember my Auntie picking wild horseradish and making this at home. Make it in a food processor, the fumes are worse than from peeling onions!

**1 large horseradish root, grated, (makes about 4 or 5 tbsp)**
**1 tbsp caster sugar**
**1 tsp mustard powder**
**2 tbsp white wine vinegar**
**150ml (¼ pint) double cream, lightly whipped**

**METHOD**
Combine all the above in a blender, and chill. Serve as an accompaniment to the sausages and Yorkshire puddings.

# Christmas is coming the goose is getting fat...

**Clarissa Porter** cooks up a wonderfully tasty Christmas lunch

## Winter salad

This is a lovely light appetiser, with a sweet sour balance of flavours, which can be tossed together in a few minutes. It combines lots of the ingredients that are always around at Christmas, or it is easily adapted to use whatever you have to hand.

Serves 6

**3 handfuls of mixed baby salad leaves (rocket, spinach, frisee and radicchio lettuce)**
**Half a jar of pickled red cabbage, drained.**
**1 lemon, and 1 orange, peeled, pipped, and sliced into rounds**
**Handful of walnuts and cobnuts**
**a few pieces of dried fruit, apple rings, prunes pre-soaked in a little water to soften**
**75g (2½oz) Stilton, crumbled**
**Walnut oil**
**Pepper**
**pumpkin seeds**

**METHOD**
Place all the ingredients in a large glass bowl, toss lightly in walnut oil, give it a few twists of the pepper mill and then sprinkle a handful of pumpkin seeds over the top.
    Serve.

C harles Dickens has a lot to answer for! He is widely credited with inventing the modern Christmas that we now celebrate. Before "A Christmas Carol" was published in 1837, Christmas was not the unbridled festival of consumption that we know today. Many people worked on Christmas Day, and though they might have gathered together for a special family meal, the day was not considered extra special. It is interesting to note that the Saxon festival of 'Yule' was celebrated over 12 days, with feasts and wassailing, pretty much like our present day Christmas. Nothing changes very much there!

But for a long time, Christmas was just another festival no more important or less important than any of the others, indeed it seems to have emerged from a combination of Halloween and Michaelmas festivities.

The traditional Michaelmas meal was goose. Goose has been part of our culture, and ancient culture for so long, that, although most of us have probably never eaten a goose, we all use goose-related phrases and sayings that hark back for centuries.

How many times have you said "it's a wild goose chase" or "don't kill the goose that lays the golden egg", or maybe: "I've got goose bumps"?

And don't forget the traditional Christmas pantomime "Mother Goose" !

In the ancient world, in countries such as Mesopotamia, geese were sacrificed as a celebration of the harvest and the change of the seasons. More recently, flocks of geese were kept and driven to market, sometimes driven great distances over several weeks before they reached the towns where the markets were held.

I expect you've all heard of the Goose Fairs held at Michaelmas, and still held in some places. Nottingham has the longest surviving Goose Fair, going back over 700 years, and interestingly, at first it was held over 12 days, mimicking the Saxon Yule Festival, which of course would have been recent history back in the 13th Century. Some 20,000 geese would arrive in Nottingham, driven from The Fens!

So the Goose was the bird of choice for a large meal or feast at any festival or family event. Queen Elizabeth is recorded as having a goose feast to celebrate the defeat of the Armada.

Turkeys didn't make their appearance in this country until 1526, when a merchant called Will Strickland brought six back from the Americas and sold them in Bristol for tuppence each.

In 2006 we brought 10 million turkeys in this country, most of them frozen. I expect nearly all of them were eaten at Christmas, I can't remember eating turkey at any other time of the year. Which is strange, since we seem to be so fond of turkey. But what really is going on, is that we are too set in our ways. We expect a large turkey as the centrepiece of our Christmas Table, and our relations, drawn together by the prospect of unbridled feasting and drinking, they expect a large turkey. I even have vegetarian friends, who although they won't eat turkey, expect to see a turkey as the centrepiece of our table. For too many people Christmas wouldn't be Christmas without a turkey! Well, this year I've decided to get back to how it used to be, back to Dicken's time when goose was the norm, and turkey was an exotic expensive dish only enjoyed by those that could afford it. The heroes of Dickens Christmas Carol, the Cratchits belonged to a "Goose Club". Goose Clubs were run by

# Ribbed cabbage with crushed juniper

A change from the ubiquitous sprouts, lovely crisp cabbage with fragrant juniper cooked in under 5 minutes

1 pointy cabbage, finely shredded into ribbons
Salt
Few juniper berries, crushed
Butter

**METHOD**
Place shredded cabbage into a pan containing a cupful of boiling salted water. Cover, and cook for no more than 4 minutes. Strain, add the crushed juniper berries, and toss in a little butter (or goose gravy).

publichouses and grocers. From the beginning of August and until Christmas, you were expected to save two sixpences a week and come Christmas Eve you'd collect your goose, and maybe a bottle of Port or Rum.

## Now, you're probably thinking," where can I buy a goose?"

Well these days it is easy. Look around your local area, ask local farm shops if any of the nearby small-holdings will be selling geese, or of course your local butcher will order one for you. Large supermarkets will have geese at Christmas, but if you're feeling adventurous you can buy geese over the internet.

There are lots of farms selling geese this way, try Google (see, even Google is pretty close to Gaggle!) but here are two farms to start with: in the Midlands, www.goodmansgeese.co.uk, and in Essex www.clerkesgeese.com.

You can collect from these farms as well, which would reduce the price. These geese will be free range domestic geese.

Before domestic geese became the norm, a wild goose was what you would expect to buy.

But these days the laws on the hunting and selling of wild goose are very strict. In fact, it is illegal to sell a wild goose that has been hunted. So unless you fancy a bit of wild fowling, or you have a friend who wild fowls, you are very unlikely to obtain a wild goose. Whereas it is OK to hunt wild geese, it is illegal to sell, exchange, or barter any wild goose! Fortunately, I have a friend who wild fowls, so I thought it would be good to try a really authentic wild goose.

The main difference between a wild and a domestic goose is the size and the fat content. Geese, being water birds have a naturally high

# Roast goose with rum

Goose is really simple to cook, the few rules are: always roast on a rack over a deep tin, so that the fat will be separate from the goose, prick the goose all over before cooking, to allow the fat to escape, and from time to time, drain off the fat during cooking, and save.

I prefer to cook the stuffing separately from the goose. Just place an apple or two, and a bay leaf, inside the goose, and maybe a squeeze of orange. This will all add to the fragrance of the finished gravy.

**1 goose, about 4.5kg (9lb)**
**salt and pepper**
**1 apple**
**1 bay leaf**
**1/2 an orange, squeezed**
**a small glass of rum, single measure**

For the Apple rum and nut stuffing
**6 eating apples, peeled, cored, chopped and soaked in rum for 2 hours.**
**3 or 4 sage leaves, finely chopped**
**Juice of half an orange**
**350g (11oz) fresh breadcrumbs**

**100g (3½oz) shelled and peeled fresh Kent cobnuts**
**175g (6oz) chestnuts, boiled for 5 minutes and peeled**

For the garnish
**3 apples, peeled,**
**1 Quince (optional)**

### METHOD
Make the stuffing the day before by combing all the ingredients for the stuffing, and either shape into balls the size of an egg, or put the lot into a buttered loaf tin. Either way, dot with a little butter. Put to one side till you are cooking the goose.

Pre heat oven to 180°C (350°F, gas 4). Remove the giblets (if present) and wipe bird with a clean damp cloth. Rub with salt and pepper inside and out. If you haven't done this already, prick all over with a fork. Place 2 apples with a bay leaf and a squeeze of orange juice into the cavity.

Place the goose on a rack inside a deep roasting dish. Cover goose with greased paper or

tinfoil over breast. Put into your pre-heated oven. From time to time, draw off the excess fat and reserve. Remove foil after about 2 and half hours - 45 minutes before the goose is cooked, add your par cooked potatoes to the remaining fat beneath the goose, also add 2 or 3 peeled apples and a quince (optional) to the fat, these will decorate the finished dish.

Place the stuffing balls on a separate greased dish and put into the oven for the last 45 minutes of the cooking period. Or if you've placed the stuffing in a loaf tin, cook for 60 minutes.

Remove goose from the oven and cover with a clean tea towel. Pile the potatoes into a warm dish. Strain off the fat leaving meat residue in the pan, add a little vegetable stock and scrape pan to deglaze. Tip into a warm gravy boat. Place your roast goose onto a large oval serving dish, and garnish with sprigs of fresh bay and sage, the roasted apples and the quince (if using), along with your roast potatoes and stuffing.

When the goose is centre stage on your table, heat some rum in a small ladle (be careful), then pour over the bird, and ignite! Serve with creamy celeriac and juniper cabbage.

fat content, like ducks. The domestic goose is slimmer at around Michaelmas, the end of September and the beginning of October. And then they are fattened for Christmas.

The wild goose is smaller and leaner, its all that flying and foraging! Goose meat is darker than turkey or chicken, and gamier to the taste.

A unique taste, I would say, and really rather special. Smaller birds are best, try to buy a bird under 10lbs. I stuffed my goose with apples soaked in rum, chestnuts, and Kentish cobnuts.

A good source of true-blue Kentish cobnuts is www.farnellfarm.co.uk in the High Weald of Kent.

One of the joys of cooking a goose is the fat can be drained and stored for later use. Roast potatoes cooked in goose fat, are famously delicious, and will ensure your guests remember this Christmas. That is what your Christmas feast should be all about, nothing brings back pleasant memories more than special meals shared with special people.

Someone once said," No one's Christmas is ever perfect, and it won't be perfect until you decide to make it reflect yourself..." In other words, try something new!     •

## "Smaller birds are best, try to buy a bird under 10lbs"

## Crisp roast potatoes

**2 large potatoes per person, peeled and sliced into quarters.**

### METHOD
Boil in salted water for about 5 minutes, drain. Toss in a little flour. Cook in hot goose fat under the goose for about 45 minutes.

# Creamy celeriac

Celeriac is a lovely fresh tasting vegetable of the celery family, I really love raw and grated with a little vinaigrette. You can prepare the following recipe omitting the potatoes, but the celeriac has a knobbly texture when mashed, and the creaminess of the mashed potato seems to bring out the flavour of the celeriac. The crispy breadcrumbs add another layer of texture and taste.

**675g (1¼lb) celeriac, peeled, and chopped into a bowl of water with a dash of lemon juice.**
**450g (15oz) potatoes, peeled and chopped**
**salt**
**50g (1½oz) butter**
**60ml single cream**

**pepper**
**handful of fresh breadcrumbs**
**knob of butter**

### METHOD
Boil the celeriac and the potatoes separately in salted water for about 20 minutes. Drain, combine, and mash together. Season with salt and pepper, and add the butter and cream. To serve, place in a pretty dish and swirl the mash with a fork to make a pyramid shape.

Melt butter in a small pan and fry breadcrumbs for a few seconds until golden, then scatter over your creamy celeriac. The celeriac can be cooked the day before and reheated.

# Nougat snow

This pudding is not quite an ice cream, not quite a nougat. But it is very delicious. It can be prepared days in advance. If you are very careful, it can be tipped out of a mould and decorated, but really, at Christmas life is too short!

I would opt for piling the nougat snow into a pretty stemmed dish or glass and topping with my candied citrus fruits (see Christmas Treats recipes). Serve as an alternative to Christmas pudding.

**100g (3½oz) flaked almonds or hazelnuts**
**50g (1½oz) icing sugar**
**300ml (½pint) double cream**
**50ml of liqueur, Grand Marnier or Amaretto**
**100g (3½oz) runny honey**
**juice of half a lemon and juice of one orange**
**50g (1½oz) caster sugar**
**6 egg whites**

### METHOD
Place nuts, generously coated with icing sugar, in oven on a medium heat for 10 minutes until caramelised. Remove, and cool slightly. Place between two sheets of greaseproof paper and bash with a rolling pin until they resemble large bread crumbs. Next, whisk cream, add liqueur and place in refrigerator.

Place honey, lemon and orange juice and the caster sugar into a pan, and melt together until boiling. Whisk egg whites until stiff.

Now for the assembly: Add the hot syrup to the egg whites, beating all the time for about 3 minutes. If you are using a hand held beater, be careful not to splash the hot syrup. Carefully slide the syrup between the whisk and the bowl to avoid splashing.

Fold in the cream and the nuts with a wooden spoon. Place in a loaf tin roughly 225mm long by 75mm high (9" x 3"). Tap the tin on a table to remove air bubbles, cover, and freeze for at least 6 hours. Serve by scooping into large wine glasses or similar and decorate with candied citrus fruit.

# The Traditional Turkey

No Christmas can be complete without a turkey sitting on the table. However, as Clarissa Porter discovered, it's not always been so

In 1526 a Yorkshireman, Will Strickland, imported and sold six turkeys for a tuppence piece each in Bristol. Ordinary country folk visiting Bristol market must have found them exciting and strangely alien. And very expensive!

No doubt people travelled from miles around to view these strange foreign birds from the other side of the world. Whether the turkeys were used for breeding or for the pot no one knows. But this was the very beginning of 'The Great Turkey Take Over'. Up until then, the bird of choice for a seasonal celebration such as Michaelmas or Christmas was the goose.

Not everyone approved of this new fangled bird. In the early 1540's someone, presumably a Puritan, wrote:

# Gilded Bronze Turkey

Gilding is a 15th Century novelty, originally real gold leaf was employed to decorate meat and poultry served at Christmas feasts. Suckling pigs, swans and peacocks were gilded and must have been amazing centre pieces at Royal tables. Sometimes the skin and feathers were removed and saved, then the bird was cooked and gilded, and the skin and feathers replaced before the dish was presented at the Royal table. As the fashion spread, the less rich developed 'endorying', a method of glazing their bird or pig imitating the extravagance of their rulers. Any fowl prepared this way was called "endored' or "endoryed".

- Bronze free-range turkey, weighing about 4.5kgs (10-11 lbs)
- Butter, a little to rub into the bird
- Sprigs of thyme and rosemary, and some string for the garland

Stuffing:
- 8 slices of good white bread
- 50g (2oz) ground almonds
- 3 shallots
- 3 sticks of celery
- peeled, cored apple or pear
- Bunch of parsley
- Sprig of sage
- tsp dried thyme
- Pepper, salt
- 2 eggs, beaten
- 50g (2oz) whole hazelnuts

For the glaze:
- 4 egg yolks
- 2 pinches of Saffron
- Little plain flour

## METHOD

To make the stuffing, whizz all the ingredients, except for the hazelnuts and eggs, together in a food processor. Tip into a bowl and add the beaten eggs and the whole hazelnuts. Mix into a ball with your hands and chill in the fridge for 20 minutes.

Wipe the turkey, and put some of the stuffing in each end. Smear the softened butter onto the turkey with your hands.

Place the bird in a foil lined turkey dish, carefully press grease proof paper over the bird. This will prevent it browning. It must adhere to the bird. Then cover the bird with two layers of foil. The idea is the bird doesn't brown before gilding. And all the juices are retained.

Cook in a pre-heated oven at 170ºC (350ºF, gas 4) for 20 minutes per 450g (1lb) weight. While the bird is cooking whisk the egg yolks, saffron and a little flour to form a paste the consistency of custard.

Remove turkey from oven, drain juices and reserve. Apply the gilding paste with a large pastry brush as evenly as you can, and not too thickly.

Return to the oven uncovered, and cook for a further 20 minutes. Remove from the oven, cover with a clean tea towel and rest for 30 minutes before carving. While it is resting make the decorative garland by twisting sprigs of thyme and rosemary together with some string into a circlet to place on top of the bird just before you bring it to your table.

I served my turkey with small cut potatoes, parsnips, sweet potato, squash, drizzled with olive oil and roasted together.

---

*'Turkeys, heresy, hops and beer;*
*Come into England,*
*All in One Year.'*

But by 1573, in Rivenhall Essex, the farmer and poet Thomas Turner, who coined the phrase: "Christmas Comes but Once a Year", wrote a poem called "Christmas Cheer":

*'Good bread and good drink, a good fire in the hall;*
*Braun, pudding and sauce, and good mustard with all;*
*Beef, mutton and pork, shred pies of the best;*
*Pig, veal, goose and capon, and Turkey well drest;*
*Cheese, apples and nuts; jolly carols to hear;*
*All these in the country are counted good cheer.'*

What a wonderful evocation of the type of traditional Christmas we long for every year!

I wonder how much two old pennies would be worth in today's money? My guess is those first turkeys must have been very expensive. How different from today! With over 17 million turkeys produced last Christmas, the price of the mass-produced turkey has fallen and fallen.

Supermarkets regularly run promotions for heavily discounted frozen turkeys. I'm rather ashamed to say that in the past I have bought a large frozen turkey for as little as £5 in one of our more upmarket supermarkets. Over the years, working as a food writer and cook, I have become more and more conscious of the responsibility we have towards these harmless birds. My husband is a photographer and we work together on food shoots, I vividly remember being telephoned in a panic by an editor from one of the colour supplements asking for an urgent Christmas food shoot. We rushed out and scoured the shops for a turkey. Finding a suitable bird we rushed home and rustled up a Christmas dinner and photographed it. Then we received a call from the same editor, panic over she said, we don't need the Christmas Dinner shot!

Something inside me was quite upset. "This bird died for nothing," I said to my husband. He wrote that down and whenever we feel ourselves doing something pointless nowadays, we look at each other and say, "this bird died for nothing'.

The turkey symbolises everything that has gone wrong with our food 'industry'. The birds produced for mass marketing are far removed from the original wild turkeys. They are bred to have the maximum amount of meat in the shortest possible life-span. So fat, they have trouble standing, let alone flying! I expect many

or you didn't know that real turkeys fly. I asked my American neighbour Dan, who is from Ohio, if he had ever seen a turkey fly. He looked at me as if I was mad! "Oh yeah" he said, "they roost in trees." He told me about a time when he was out riding his motorbike, and coming round a bend there was a turkey in the middle of the road. The bird ran towards him, taking off just in time to clear Dan and his bike!

Turkeys are native to North America; fossil remains have been discovered that are 10 million years old. The Indians had domesticated and interbred different varieties centuries before the Spanish explorers arrived. North American Indians used the feathers in their head-dresses and as flights on their arrows. They sometimes used the spurs as arrow tips. The Spanish brought them from Mexico to Spain in 1498, and from there they spread across Europe. Early 17th Century English settlers to America would have been well acquainted with turkeys; in fact they took the birds with them from England!

Historically they were eaten all year round, smaller in the summer and growing larger in autumn and winter. They were killed in the autumn because their owners couldn't afford to feed them over the winter. Conveniently that meant they were ready for the Thanksgiving and Christmas feasts, and so the tradition was established almost accidentally of eating turkey at Christmas.

You could say that historically there was 'Turkey' and then there was 'Christmas Turkey'!

Forget for a moment mass-produced supermarket turkeys, let's talk real turkey. The older the bird, the tastier it will be; smaller birds are better than larger birds; cookbooks from the 18th and 19th Centuries specify a turkey of around 6lbs. A 'real' turkey will be able to fly, in fact it will have to fly in order to survive, and it will be 'single-breasted'. A real turkey will have had a varied diet, mostly from foraging. There are many varieties of traditional turkey, the best known being the 'Bronze' which came about in 1830 in Rhode Island by crossing wild turkeys with a domesticated variety the Narragansett. There are several types of Bronze, some have been bred to be broad-breasted, but original Bronzes are 'un-imposed'.

What an apt word that is regarding turkeys. Mass production has imposed unnatural feeding and living conditions on these unfortunate birds. They are bred on an artificial, chemically enhanced diet in order to fit what the supermarkets think we want. Sometime in the 1950's and 1960's, the producers decided that housewives 'wanted' antiseptic uniform birds that bear no relation to the Wild Turkey. The result is that modern turkeys have very short lives. They are sterile and sedentary, living on a fixed diet pumped full of growth hormones in crowded conditions, bred to be 'double-breasted', and generically known as the 'Broad Breasted White'. Flavourless physical wrecks in fact. And don't even get me started on the infamous Turkey Twizzler that once made up our school dinner menus!

Fortunately, we don't have to conform to the supermarket's idea of 'what housewives want'. Which would you prefer: taste, or a bird that cuts like butter with no taste? There are plenty of producers of traditional birds; you just have to use a little effort finding them. The internet is a starting point; you could try contacting the Turkey Club: www.turkeyclub.org.uk and your local farm or smallholder may raise a few traditional turkeys. The average back garden could

# Prune and Marzipan Tart

This one of my favourite tarts, simpl[e]
ingredients make a tart that is somehow ver[y]
classy, just right for the Christmas table[.]
Even friends that profess not to like prune[s]
can't stop themselves coming back for more[.]

### Ingredients
250g (9oz) creme fraich[e]
2 egg[s]

### For the custard filling
50g (2oz) caster suga[r]
50g (2oz) ground almond[s]
250g (9oz) pitted prune[s]
A little brand[y]
A little marzipa[n]

### For the pastry
100g (4oz) plain flou[r]
Pinch of sa[lt]
40g (1½oz) ground almond[s]
40g (1½oz) caster suga[r]
1 egg yolk, beate[n]
vanilla essenc[e]
75g (3oz) butte[r]

### METHO[D]
First soak the pitted prunes in a little brand[y.]
Then make the pastry, place all the pastr[y]
ingredients in a food processor and whiz[z]
together until they form a ball. Don't over do th[e]
whizzing or the mixture will become oil[y.]
Remove and chill for 30 minutes. Then roll ou[t]
and line a 22.5cm (8in) diameter loose-ring ta[rt]
tin. Bake blind for 25 minutes in an oven a[t]
180ºC (350ºF, gas 4[)]
Remove and cool. While it is cooling whis[k]
together all the custard ingredients. Drain th[e]
prunes and add the brandy to the custard. Ro[ll]
out bean sized pieces of marzipan and stu[ff]
into each prune. Then arrange prunes in th[e]
tart shel[l.]
Pour over the custard and place the tart t[in]
on a baking tray. Put back in the oven for abou[t]
40 minutes until the custard has set and i[s]
golden. Remove from the oven, cool, then dus[t]
with icing sugar and serve. Fantasti[c!]

accommodate a pair of these friendly majestic birds; why not keep your own?

This is very important; you can help preserve heritage turkeys just by eating them! If there was no demand, then only a few enthusiasts would raise them for their own pleasure. I can't emphasise this enough, we will lose these traditional breeds if we don't demand them, we must support small poultry farmers before they disappear forever. And since they were historically eaten all the year round, why restrict yourself to just one Turkey a year? They make excellent light summer eating, and because of their size even the most expensive birds are really good value.

Our publisher Stephen, a man who practices what he preaches in "Country kitchen", raises his own Bronze Turkeys bred from a wild strain. He rears them slowly and naturally, and yes they can fly! The hens (females) are better fliers than the toms (males), and like to roost in trees to be away from the foxes. Stephen had to trim the hens' feathers; they had become too adventurous, an[d] were escaping over the two metre high fence! H[e] gave me one of his turkeys for my Christma[s] recipe, it was very good, exactly how a prope[r] turkey should taste. His birds live at least twice a[s] long as mass-produced birds, and they have th[e] freedom to perch and peck where they choose[.] After they are killed, they are hung for four day[s] before eating which enhances the flavour. An[d] what a flavour, you only live once, order [a] 'heritage' turkey!

# Christmas treats

## For those unexpected visitors, and perhaps as presents, sweet treats are handy to have ready, just in case!, says *Clarisssa Porter*

They will also fill your home with sweet aromas and colour. Like dishes from medieval feasts, they are designed to surprise and entertain your guests. A little love and care in preparing something special, no matter how simple will be appreciated by your guests, and be a welcome change from the tin of biscuits or boiled sweets. The children will love helping you prepare the sugar mice, but keep them away from the chocolate salami! It is Adults Only!

## Candied citrus fruit

With all the oranges, lemons and other citrus fruits around at Christmas time, it is such a shame to waste the peel, when it can be turned into something very sophisticated in 20 minutes, or so. Wonderful on it's own, or with ice cream, and a classy decoration for many puddings.

**Citrus peelings, oranges, lemons, limes, grapefruit**
**900ml (11/2pint) boiling water**

Stock syrup

**100g (3½oz) caster sugar**
**100ml 3fl oz) water**
**half a lemon**

**METHOD**
Cut peel into strips, try to keep some continuous whirls. Remove as much pith as possible. Simmer in boiling water for 4 minutes. Remove and drain. Make stock syrup by boiling sugar, water and lemon, until the sugar dissolves. Place peel into the stock syrup and boil for 3 or 4 minutes. Tip out onto a baking tray and allow to cool. Store covered until needed.

# Coconut ice

A blast from the past! A favourite with all my aunties! Try making it with the very best ingredients so that you can taste the difference from the inferior shop bought product.

**900g (1¾lb) golden granulated sugar**
**250ml (8fl oz) organic milk**
**25g (¾oz) butter**
**a little vanilla essence**
**225g (7oz) organic desiccated coconut**
**a little red food colour**

## METHOD
Place the milk, butter and sugar in a pan and boil for 10 minutes. Remove from the heat, add the coconut, vanilla and beat until creamy. Line a tin with greaseproof paper, pour in half the mixture. Colour the remaining mixture with the food colour, a pour on top of the mixture already in the tin. Place in a fridge to set.

# Christmas mice

A bit of fun for the children. If they get bored, hide them around the house for a game of Mousey Hide'n'Seek. Or you can use them as place markers for your Christmas table. The children will love helping make these treats.

**450g (14½oz) icing sugar, and maybe a little extra for rolling.**
**1 or 2 egg whites**
**2 capfuls of peppermint essence (or Creme de Menthe if they are for grown-ups)**
**Silver cake decorating balls for eyes**
**String for the tails.**

## METHOD
Combine sugar, egg whites and peppermint essence to make a thick shiny pastry like paste. Place in fridge for 10 minutes. Powder a flat surface with icing sugar. Roll out a long sausage of the mixture (with clean hands). Slice into about lengths of about 40mm (egg size). Roll each piece into a ball, pinch one end to make the nose, take two pea size pieces from the roll and squeeze between thumb and forefinger to make ears. Squidge into mouse shape at ear level. Use two silver balls for the eyes, and cut a length of string and push in to make the tail. Store in a very cool place until needed.

# Chocolate salami

These have to be tasted to be believed! Every Christmas I make about 30 to give as presents. I am not allowed to stop making them! My friend's eyes light up at the mere mention of them, but, beware, they are not for children! And they are not cheap. To make one salami, which is enough for 6 people (perhaps!)

**350g (11oz) very good plain chocolate**
**225g (7oz) unsalted butter**
**2 egg yolks**
**4 tbsp of Amaretto liqueur**
**12 malted biscuits, crushed**
**12 Amaretti biscuits, crushed**
**50g (1½oz) toasted flaked almonds**
**a few ground almonds and crushed amaretti biscuits to finish**

## METHOD
Melt the butter, chocolate and the liqueur in a bowl set over a pan of gently boiling water. Stir. When it is smooth and liquid, remove from the heat, cool slightly, and beat in the egg yolks. Stir in the crushed biscuits and nuts. Set aside to cool until it thickens so that it is similar to pastry. Spread onto doubled greaseproof paper into a salami sausage shape about 300 mm long. Using the greaseproof paper, roll up like a Christmas cracker, to smooth. Place in fridge to cool a little more, maybe for 5 minutes. Remove and unwrap. Roll your sausage in a mixture of crushed biscuit and ground almonds. Wrap in paper, I use greaseproof paper and string, and red ribbon, so that it closely resembles a real salami. Serve, chilled, sliced thinly, with maybe coffee, at the end of a meal.

# Poultry and game soup

by *Clarissa Porter*

There is nothing more appetizing than the aroma of a steaming bowl of home-made soup, made with real stock, and Christmas is the ideal time to get stock-making, because there will be loads of leftovers from the orgy of eating!

Imagine returning from a long country walk, trying to work off the Christmas waistline, to a beautiful bowl of warming soup, and the smell of fresh warm bread (you've baked yourself!), and a glass or two of good wine...

There are only a couple of rules to successful stock-making. Never use old, dry, stale meat carcasses, freeze leftovers till you're ready to make your stock, and never over-cook it, the result will appear cloudy, and have a horrid 'bone' flavour. Otherwise, be creative and use what you have to hand, which at Christmas should be no problem! A tub of veal stock (available in any good supermarket), and wine are the classic stock enhancers, but even a very simple stock adds depth of flavour to soup, and is really worth the effort. ●

## Making the stock

### Poultry stock

**Turkey/chicken carcass, neck, feet, leftover meat, whatever you have**
**2 onions, halved, 2 carrots, 2 sticks of celery**
**1 large bouquet-garni (bunch of bay, thyme, parsley)**
**A little olive oil or groundnut oil.**
**Salt and pepper.**

### Game stock

Substitute pheasant or guinea fowl, or whatever you have, instead of poultry.

**METHOD**
With the poultry you can either lightly brown the meat and vegetables in the oil before covering with water, or simply cover everything generously with water (you'll need a very big pan!). Simmer for about an hour, then strain.

For the game stock, proceed as above but using pheasant, pigeon, Guinea fowl or whatever you have to hand. A glass, or maybe even several, of good red wine is a vast improvement, although of course you'll need less water. The quantity of water needed is governed by how many leftovers you have, always cover generously!

# Mulled roast tomato and game soup

**1 litre (2 pints) of game stock**
**1 red onion, quartered**
**1 bulb of garlic, halved**
**1kg (2 lbs) medium size ripe tomatoes**
**1 clove for each tomato**
**1 bay leaf**
**1 cinnamon stick**
**Olive oil**
**Pepper and salt**
**Pinch of sugar**
**Port, a small glass**
**Any leftover game meat you might have...**

**METHOD**
Place the tomatoes, each stuck with a clove in a baking tin along with the onion, garlic, bay, and cinnamon stick. Season with salt and pepper, and drizzle with olive oil. Cook for about 30 minutes in a pre-heated oven at 190°C/375°F/Gas 5, until the tomato skins have split, and the kitchen smells wonderfully! Remove from the oven, allow to cool enough for you to peel and remove the core from the tomatoes. Discard the cloves, cinnamon stick, bay leaf, and onion.

Then liquidize the tomatoes and garlic along with the juices from the baking tin and adding some of the game meat to the liquidizer. Pour into a clean saucepan, and add enough game stock to make fairly thick soup. It will have a slightly coarse texture because of the game. Add a small glass of port, heat through, and serve in warm bowls with little mounds of the reserved game meat in the centre of each bowl.

Grate a little nutmeg to taste, and serve with hunks of bread. This is a really rich, grown-up soup!

# Turkey and sweet potato chowder

**1.5 litres (1½ to 2 pints) of turkey/chicken stock**
**50g (2 oz) butter**
**4 medium sweet potatoes, sliced**
**4 potatoes, sliced**
**1 onion chopped**
**350g sweetcorn**
**Single cream**
**Nutmeg**

## METHOD

Into a saucepan, melt the butter, add the onion and then the potatoes. After about a minute, add enough stock to just cover the ingredients. Cover the pan with a lid and simmer until the potatoes are tender. You don't need copious amounts of liquid at this stage, if you do not have much of your precious stock you could use water to cook the vegetables, and then use the stock to finish. Drain, and then liquidize the potatoes and the corn. Return to a clean pan, and add enough stock to make a fairly thick soup. Add a good dash of cream, heat through, and serve with a swirl of cream, and a sprinkle of nutmeg.

Children in particular will love this soup.

# Chestnut and celery soup

**1 litre (2 pints) of chicken/turkey stock**
**50g (2 oz) butter**
**1 head of celery (the whole bunch)**
**1 tin of chestnuts (peeled, whole)**
**1 onion finely diced**
**Sage leaves**

## METHOD

This simple soup relies on very good chicken stock. Remove the stringy bits from the celery with a peeler, and slice diagonally into 2cm (1 inch) diamonds. Melt the butter in a saucepan, add the onions, cook but do not brown. Add the celery and just cover with the stock. Cover saucepan with lid, and poach till the celery is tender, don't let the liquid boil! Add the chestnuts and a couple of sage leaves, and more stock. Allow to heat through, and serve with a fresh sage leaf.

# Snowed Under

It really is amazing what you can do with a few store cupboard essentials, a leg of lamb, a chicken and some bread as **Clarissa Porter** explains

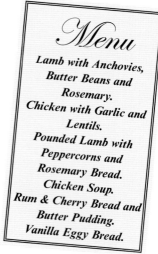

## Lamb with anchovies, butter beans and rosemary

Rosemary grows abundantly around the shacks on the beach, other herbs are affected by the winds and heat of the summer, but rosemary is a survivor! Cooking 6 legs of lamb for the crew meant I needed loads, but I can report the bush survived my plundering. I have scaled down the recipe to family proportions.

Serves 4

1 leg of lamb, about 2-2.5kgs (4-5lb)
1 tin of anchovies
1 lemon
Fresh rosemary, a big bunch
3 tins of butter beans
garlic
pepper, salt
Olive oil
Pinch of sugar

### METHOD

Wipe the lamb with a sheet of kitchen towel. Place in a roasting tin on top of a large piece of rosemary. Make small slashes in the meat and poke in slices of garlic. Squeeze the juice of 1 lemon over the meat. Arrange the anchovies on the top surface of the meat. Season with salt, pepper, and a pinch of sugar.

Place in the oven preheated to 220°C (425°F, gas 7) and cook for 20 minutes, then reduce the heat to 180°C (350°F, gas 4) and cook for a further 60 minutes.

I think a leg of lamb is best slightly undercooked, but you should use your own judgement. Remove the lamb from the oven and the tin, and cover with a tea towel for 20 minutes. Add the drained butter beans to the tin and return to the oven for as long as necessary to warm through. Serve, with the lamb surrounded by the butter beans and juices.

For the film crew I served with crispy roast parsnips and roast squash.

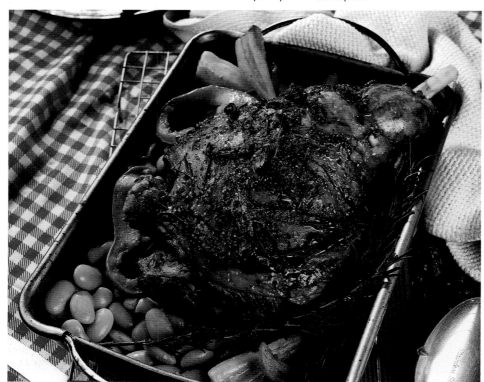

long the North Kent coast there is a beach of sand and shells, stretching out into the Thames Estuary. It is a wild, remote and forgotten place. Ten shacks are arranged haphazardly on the beach at the waters edge, the remains of a once thriving fishing community. The only access from the land is along an unmade track about half a mile long, which at this time of the year is deeply rutted and flooded. We are lucky enough to own one of these shacks. A couple of years ago, I was contacted by a film company. The cheery voice at the other end of the line enquired if they could use the shack for a scene in a film they were making. With the sound of cash registers ringing in my ears, I agreed to meet the director at the beach the following weekend to discuss the arrangements.

We met on the Saturday afternoon, it was bitterly cold and bleak. There were four of them, Mark the director, Phil the writer, Michael the producer, and Hoi the assistant. It quickly became obvious that it was not a big budget production. When I broached the subject of money there was some uneasy sideways glances and shuffling of feet, and mutterings of, 'well we're working for nothing you know...'

How long do you want it for we asked, "Oh, about a couple of days". "How many people?" "Oh, about half a dozen". What's the film about? "Oh, it's a vampire film," said Phil the writer, rather defensively. "It's a very popular genre," he went on, rather unconvincingly.

And so on.

We settled on a fee, about half what I had been hoping for, and then I relaxed. Michael (the moneyman) said something about having to feed the crew, and because of the remoteness of the beach, where was the nearest sandwich shop?

This was when I made my big mistake. "I could make some sandwiches," I offered. They leapt at this, and promised to call us later in the week with further details and dates.

When the call came, it was from Hoi. She left a message on our answer phone, "We'll need the

# Chicken with garlic and lentils

I somehow managed to cook 6 of these in my seaside kitchen. It just goes to show what can be achieved with even the simplest of kitchens if you put your mind to it. Despite the garlic, the 'vampires' loved it.

Serves 4

1 chicken 1.75-1.9kgs, free range of course.
5 heads of garlic
Fresh thyme
1 lemon
olive oil
3 tins of lentils
pepper and salt
900g (2lb) potatoes, peeled
butter
cream

## METHOD

Wipe the chicken, put half a lemon and some thyme into the cavity and place in a roasting tin. The lemon has antiseptic qualities as well as adding flavour. Lay thyme and halved garlic heads around the chicken. Squeeze the remaining lemon juice over the dish, then season the chicken with salt and pepper and drizzle over some olive oil.

Cook in an oven preheated to 220°C (425°F, gas 7) for 20 minutes per 450g ((1lb)), plus an additional 20 minutes. Just before the last 20 minutes, drain the tinned lentils, and place the lentils around the chicken. If you have any sherry handy, a splash added at this point would be good. Return the chicken to the oven for the final 20 minutes. Now boil the potatoes and mash with cream and pepper. Remove a little of the garlic, maybe a few cloves, and mash them into the potato as well. Remove the chicken from the oven, cover and allow to stand for 5 minutes.

Arrange the mash around the chicken and serve.

location from Tuesday to Friday, the last week of February. There will be 22 people in the crew, and they will need 3 meals a day, starting with breakfast at 8am. They will need drinks and snacks available throughout the day." Alarm bells rang, actually they pealed deafeningly.

You see, these shacks are just that, shacks. There is no electricity, no water, just bottled gas, oil lamps and candles. There are water butts to collect water from the roof, and there is a loo... of sorts!

I made an anguished call to Hoi: "I can't do this on £50," I squealed. £50 was the sum agreed for the sandwiches. Hoi seemed surprised. "And I will need to rent another of the shacks just to cook and serve 22 people."

Hoi sounded crestfallen. She said she'd have to call me back.

When the call came she sounded slightly more cheerful, the producer had agreed an additional budget for the catering.

We arranged to rent another shack about 50 yards down the beach. We would stay there and cook, and the crew could use it as abase.

The Sunday before the start, we shopped for the first two days.

We arrived at the beach on the Monday laden with legs of lamb, some chicken, the basics to cook with, acres of paper napkins, and a ton of chocolate biscuits. The plan was to go to the remarkable farm shop in Brambledown, as and when we needed further supplies, a distance of about 16 miles there and back. There is also a surprisingly excellent bakery in nearby Leysdown that bakes their own bread and cakes, and we could rely on them for fresh bread and croissants.

I prepared the cooking area. Imagine a galley type arrangement, an ancient gas cooker running off propane, a sink with only ice cold water, and no mod cons at all! To light the oven, you have to get on your hands and knees and reach into the bowels of the ancient beast with a lit match as the gas hisses (the knack is to do this as fast as possible if you want to retain your eyebrows.).

Sporadic yellow flames leap up at the back of the oven, and they remain unaltered by the controls, they are either on or off.

My husband, David, walked the lurcher and prepared our shack for the crew: wooden shutters had to be removed from the windows and the toilet cleaned, and little notes left to guide the sophisticated townies as to the correct behaviour under these alien (to them) circumstances, "Don't Attempt To Light A Tilley Lamp Without Help' and 'Don't Put Anything Down The Loo Except What's Meant To Go Down, Signed the septic tank police' etc.

We spent a pleasant if chilly night, relaxed and confident.

Next morning, David went to the bakery to buy fresh bread for breakfast. A few snow flakes drifted down from an increasingly grey sky. The crew arrived, they had rented caravans in a nearby holiday camp. That first morning everything went very well, our confidence buoyed with the thought that 'we can do this!' The crew seemed very appreciative of our efforts, saying that up until now on this film they'd had to make do with 'greasy spoons' near to wherever they were filming in London.

But the snowflakes had turned into a blizzard, and soon the beach and the surrounding area was deep in snow, something we had never experienced at the beach before. The temperature had dropped dramatically. The crew rigged up an enormous generator and circled our shack with lights.

Eventually they called it a day, and after eating very well departed down the track. The snow was still falling, and so was the temperature. We boiled water and did the washing-up listening to the local radio station. Trains were being cancelled, schools were closed, and hospitals were requesting help from the Gurkhas stationed at Canterbury.

That night was too cold to sleep in the unheated bedroom, so we slept on the floor in sleeping bags in front of the wood burner, the lurcher joined us gratefully.

Next morning dawned very grey and cold, the track looked impassible, but soon the minibus bringing the crew came into view sliding about down the track. 22 shivering people came for breakfast. We began to worry about our plans to fetch fresh supplies. Anxiously we listened to the radio to see if there was any end in sight to the unexpectedly severe weather.

But all we heard was a repeated litany of schools closed and karate lessons in church halls cancelled. And still it snowed. David had to keep shovelling snow from the seawall between the two shacks, so that the crew could walk backwards and forwards safely. The floors in the shacks had become slippery with melted snow and an air of resignation hung in the air. The temperature dropped further, and the water butts froze. We had to get buckets of sea water to flush the toilets. That night as we lay on the floor in front of the wood burner, we had an anxious re-appraisal of how we could continue feeding 22 people and ourselves without further supplies. The radio reported that the temperature that night was minus 11 centigrade, the coldest and worst weather in Kent for over 50 years.

Next morning we woke to the strangest sight, the surface of the sea had frozen, and was lazily sloshing backwards and forwards like a slush puppy. Some members of the crew made a snowman on the beach, and as the tide came in, the snowman floated out to sea, more or less intact. Then an emergency, the camerawoman Nemone couldn't move one of her fingers, Hoi diagnosed frostbite!

I could feel an air of panic descending on the crew. For the first time they seemed to lose their cheerful confidence. An emergency trip to the cottage hospital in the four wheeldrive reassured everybody, Nemone's finger was just in a very advanced state of numbness. Two girls arrived out of the blue from London, they had come to shoot 'extras' for the DVD.

Their arrival cheered everyone up, I asked how they'd managed the trip from London in an old Fiat Uno, "We're from Canada," they said. "This is nothing!" And later they went back! I rang friends in London, it was fine there apparently, no snow at all.

The snow had stopped, but everything was deep frozen, and the sky was battleship grey. It was so icy that the actors walking to and from the two shacks had to be escorted so that they didn't slip. Somehow they managed to finish filming that night, and just in time, the food having all but run out. The next morning the sun was out and the snow had begun to thaw. The crew returned to recover their equipment and say their farewells. Watch out for the film, Hoi says it will be released this year, its called 'Vampire Diaries'. Hoi said they had to rewrite some of the script to account for the weather! Now here are some of the recipes I cooked that wintery week, making do with supplies that were meant to last for two days. I have of course scaled down the amounts to serve four people. But this is simple, basic filling stuff. And I hope warming for the time of year!  •

# Pounded lamb with peppercorns and rosemary bread

After roasting 5 legs of lamb for the crew, there were plenty of leftovers not to be wasted.

So with my trusty granite pestle and mortar I set about pounding the leftovers into this teatime snack. Spread on warm rosemary oven toast it was a hit with the crew, who could eat it on the move.

Serves 4

**350g (12oz) lamb meat cut into small cubes**
**Juice of half a lemon**
**2 anchovies**
**3 cloves of cooked garlic**
**1 tbsp crushed black peppercorns**
**50g (2oz) butter, melted**

**METHOD**
Put your lamb, lemon juice, garlic and anchovies, together with a little of the oil the anchovies came in, into your pestle.

You may only have a small pestle so, mix the above together and put a little at a time into the pestle. Then pound the mixture into a pate type of consistency. Place into a pate dish or a large ramekin, or a jelly mould. Scatter the crushed peppercorns and pour over the melted butter. Put in the fridge to set (or in my case on the window ledge outside).

Serve with oven toast: simply slice good white bread and then poke in a few sprigs of fresh rosemary. Place in a hot oven till crisp and serve. A few pickled gherkins would be good too!

# Vanilla eggy bread

From leftover bread, a few apples and some eggs... What shall I make? Then it came to me, something from my childhood brought up to date. When the going gets tough, we all yearn for comfort food !

**1 slice of white bread per person**
**1 egg per person, beaten with a little sugar, milk or cream, and a dash of vanilla essence per person**
**Butter, for frying**
**2 apples per person**
**Sugar**
**Brandy, just a dash.**

**METHOD**
Slice the bread (if necessary).

Beat together the egg, cream (or milk), sugar and dash of vanilla and set aside.

Peel and slice the apples, and in a saucepan cook with a little sugar and a little butter until soft, but not mushy. Add a dash of brandy. Dip the slices bread in the egg mixture you set aside, and fry until golden.

Then serve topped with 2 or 3 spoonfuls of the apple, and maybe dust with icing sugar.

If you are doing a large quantity, the fried bread can be kept warm in the oven.

# Chicken soup

Six chickens later, I had plenty of leftovers to make a really good stock. With some butter beans, a bunch of spinach, and a tin of coconut milk I found at the back of the cupboard, all I needed was a big pot and a wood burning stove. Chicken soup is good for the soul, as the book says!

Serves 4 - 6

**Chicken carcass, remove any pieces of chicken**
**1 carrot**
**1 stick of celery**
**1 onion**
**Spinach**
**leftover butter beans**
**water**

### METHOD

Using a large saucepan, place all of the ingredients in the pan and cover with water. Heat and bring to the boil, simmer gently for no longer than 1 hour. Strain the liquid into another saucepan, add any pieces of chicken leftovers. Add any butter beans leftover from the lamb dish, some spinach and a tin of coconut milk. Taste, and adjust seasoning with salt and pepper. If necessary you could add a little chicken stock powder.

Serve with some good bread.

# Rum and cherry bread and butter pudding

With all the bread and croissants left over from breakfasts, the obvious thing to do was to make an enormous bread and butter pudding. So I used a turkey tin! And I threw in some extras, rum and tinned cherries. This went down a treat with the crew.

It was just right for a cold snowy day. One of the earliest puddings, inexpensive and filling and easily adapted to your own larder. I first cooked this for a Victorian themed photo shoot in the farmhouse at the Beamish Museum. We cooked it on a wood-powered cast iron range at 6 O'clock in the morning, before the museum opened! Ever since then, this has been a firm favourite in my house.

Serves 4

**450ml (16fl oz) full cream milk**
**450ml (16fl oz) double cream**
**1 vanilla pod (or essence ) or 1 cinnamon stick**
**3 eggs, beaten**
**125g (4½oz) sugar**
**8 slices of white bread, best if it is not too fresh, crusts removed**
**(you can use croissants)**
**50g (2oz) butter**
**1 tin of pitted cherries, drained**
**75g (3oz) sultanas**
**Rum, or brandy**

### METHOD

Butter an ovenproof dish, a 1 pint (500ml) pie dish, a rectangular shape is good I think. Butter the slices of bread, cut into triangles and arrange across the bottom of the dish. Finish with a layer of bread, butter side up. Soak the cherries and sultanas in a little rum. Beat the eggs, milk and sugar together with a little vanilla essence. (On the day when I made the vast pud I added a little custard powder to the mixture). If you are using a vanilla pod or a stick of cinnamon, place them snugly into the bread in the bottom of the dish. Pour the fruit and rum over the bread, then pour in the egg and milk and sugar mixture. And then leave to stand for 1 hour, this is the secret of a good bread and butter pudding. Put a few dots of butter around, then place in the top of an oven pre-heated to medium heat, about 180°C (350°F, gas 4). Cook for about 40 minutes until the top is golden and crispy.

Serve, warm not hot, dusted with icing sugar, and maybe a little nutmeg.

# A month of Sundays

Why is it that February is the shortest month of the year, yet it always seems to be the longest? **Clarissa Porter** has the answer!

## Standing rib of beef with Yorkshire pudding

Serves 6 – 8

This impressive Olde English dish will feed an army of family and friends! Originally served with beer, but around the beginning of the eighteenth century a 'dripping pudding' was invented in Yorkshire. This ousted beer as the traditional accompaniment. The standing rib is truly robust and traditional, a magnificent centre piece for your table.

**6kg (12lb) standing rib of beef (you may prefer a smaller rib)**
**2tbs flour**
**1tbs mustard powder**
**fresh ground black pepper**

For the Yorkshire puddings
**150g (5oz) flour**
**1 large egg, beaten**
**300 ml (½pt) milk**
**pinch of salt**

### METHOD

For the beef, mix the mustard powder with the 2 tablespoons of flour, add a little pepper, then rub the mixture into the fat of the beef. Heat a little dripping or oil in your roasting pan, and quickly seal all of the beef, but NOT the fat. You can now season the meat of the beef. Place in your preheated oven (200°C, 400°F gas 6) for 15 minutes per 450g (1lb), and an extra 20 minutes.

Meanwhile, prepare the pudding batter, sift the flour into a bowl. Make a hollow in the centre and add the egg and salt. Then stirring slowly, add the milk. Keep stirring and beating with a fork till you have a smooth creamy batter. There must be no lumps! Cover with a clean dry tea towel and place some where cool to rest for at least 30 minutes. This allows any air in the batter to escape. When the beef is cooked, remove from the oven and allow it to rest. Drain off a little of the dripping in the pan. For the Yorkshire puddings I used muffin tins, each tin has 6 moulds. Put a teaspoon of the dripping into each mould and place the tin into your oven for about 5 minutes till the dripping is so hot it smokes. Then remove the tin from the oven and quickly spoon in some batter into each mould, 1 or 2 tablespoons into each mould. It doesn't matter that it seems too little! Place the tin back in the oven for another 25 minutes or so. If your oven has a glass door you can judge how long. The batter will rise and turn golden brown. Resist opening the door for a look! This is a good moment to make some gravy.

When the puddings are done, serve heaped around the beef. I like to serve the beef with fresh horseradish and English mustard. I know you will be talking about this Sunday dinner for weeks.

Remember, "Beef and Liberty!"

After all the optimism of the New Year, with our lists of resolutions and plans for the future, before you know it, it's February. I used to think of February as almost Spring, but nowadays it is usually the coldest, most snowy month of the Winter. Spring has to wait till March, or even April.

And so, if any month ever deserved the dubious accolade of 'a month of Sundays', then surely February is that month.

A good way to cheer yourself up is to have something to look forward to. So I thought I would set myself a project incorporating one of my New Year Resolutions. Along with losing weight, taking more exercise and watching less TV, I had resolved that: "I must see more of my family (and friends)".

One of the best ways of achieving this, I thought, would be to invite them for Sunday dinner. A roast Sunday dinner harks back to a relatively recent time in our history, when most people worked six days a week. Sunday, the day of rest, was the only day when the whole family could be together. The best meal of the week was always the Sunday dinner, the budget being eked out to allow for a splendid feast before the start of another arduous week. In those not so distant days, cooking methods were decidedly primitive by today's standards. Around 150 years or so ago, families would be cooking on a coal or wood-fired range if they were lucky, and the joint of meat would probably have been roasted on a spit. I've mentioned before my day cooking in the restored farmhouse at Beamish Museum in County Durham. The main dish I prepared was a large joint of beef. At the time, about ten years ago, it was the biggest joint I had ever bought or cooked. I remember it cost about £30 even then. It was huge! I attached it to a vertical spit which was operated by a complicated clockwork chain and pulley mechanism, rather like a fast-running grandfather clock. This turned the spit slowly in front of hot coals behind a grill, and it was possible to adjust the distance of the meat from the hot coals.

The spit had to be rewound from time to time, and the range had to be fed with coal. It would have been a full time job using one of theses ranges. It took all day to cook the joint, and it shrank considerably, but the farm workers seemed to enjoy it!

This was a very educational experience, and I've never forgotten how difficult and time consuming everyday life must have been for people back then. It really brought home to me the slow pace of life in the 19th century. It was impossible to do anything, especially cook, at anything like the speed of today. My whole day was planned and began at 5am with lighting of the range and the 'copper' (for the laundry).

So, you see how the leisurely pace of a traditional Sunday roast came about. It would take literally all day to cook, and therefore it was a meal that could only be undertaken on the day of rest, when perhaps the whole family would be at home.

I think you'll agree, that when people say "I fancy a roast" they actually mean sitting around a table having a big comforting meal, with lots of different vegetables, homely and hot, with a splendid centre piece of roast meat or chicken.

For our household this usually means the centre piece is a roast chicken, because chicken is universally liked by young and old alike. Then I thought, "hang on, I don't want to be cooking

# Pheasant in a plum tree

Serves 4–6

This dish is rustic and posh all at once, and it takes no time at all to prepare. Did you know that Pheasants originally came from China? But they have been resident here since Roman times. Buying your birds from a reputable game dealer will ensure they have been hung for the correct time, these days hanging times are considerably shorter than they were in years gone by.

**A brace (2) of pheasants, my brace weighed 1.75kg (2lb 8oz)**
**6 slices of streaky bacon**
**Thyme, lots!**
**8 plums, stoned and cut into quarters. If you can't get fresh use tinned**
**Butter**
**Sugar to taste**
**Cinnamon stick**
**Lemon juice**
**Pepper**

### METHOD
Place Pheasants, wrapped in the bacon, in a roasting tin. There is no need to seal them because of the bacon. Scatter them with Thyme and pepper. Place the tin in a preheated oven at 180°C (350°F, gas 4) for about 30 minutes. Meanwhile, gently place the plums, sugar, butter, and Cinnamon in a pan till butter and sugar melt and plums begin to cook.

They should not go squishy so be gentle. Taste and adjust with lemon juice or maybe more sugar. You could add a little red wine or port, but it isn't imperative. Serve the pheasants with a little of the aromatic plum sauce. A surprising but simple side dish would be game chips made from celeriac instead of potatoes.

The countryside on a plate!

# Belly of pork with prunes and pears

Serves 6

This is the most economical of my Sunday dinners. The gravy you can make from the fruity meat juices is out of this world! Like all the other dishes, this is a visual feast as well, so give it a try, you won't be disappointed!

**2.5 - 3 kg (6lb) Belly of pork, boned. (If you buy from a butcher, he will bone the pork, you can keep the ribs for another day)**
**20 pitted prunes**
**1 large firm pear, cored and diced, skin on**
**2 or more pears to roast whole alongside**
**Fresh sage**
**a little Calvados or Brandy**
**Pepper and salt**
**Pinch of sugar**
**a little oil**
**string**

## METHOD

Put the chopped pears and the prunes in a little Brandy to soak. Wipe the skin of the pork so that it is really dry. Hopefully your butcher will have scored the skin for you, otherwise, using a really sharp knife (butchers use a Stanley knife) score the skin. Run salt and oil into the skin to make good crackling. Turn over and season the underside with pepper and salt and a little sugar. Then scatter onto the meat the chopped pears and prunes, and some sage. Roll up the pork, and tie with string along the length in several places. Place in a baking tin, if you like place some whole scored pears alongside, they will add to the gravy, and they certainly add to the presentation of the dish. Place in a preheated oven at 200°C (400°F, gas 6) and time the cooking as before with the beef. Test with askewer. Remove from the oven and allow to rest, meanwhile make your gravy. I promise you the gravy will be really special! Serve with may be roast or mashed parsnips. Try not to fight over the crackling!

chicken for the entire month of February!" I usually cook chicken more than once a week as it is, so I decided to plan four different Sunday roasts, trying to avoid the most predictable cuts of meat. And not one would be the ubiquitous bird!

The first three were easy, roast beef of course, roast lamb, and roast pork. The three staples of a Sunday pub lunch. I confess I dithered about the fourth, we had roast goose at Christmas, and it was excellent, I would have had another goose, but goose is a 'grown-up' taste, some of the children didn't like it, and there were complaints from Granny who thinks goose is exotic. I also would have liked a roast fish, Salmon perhaps, or Sea Bream. But in the end, I decided to compromise and cook a brace of pheasants. The pheasant shooting season ends on February 1st, but there's still plenty available at the beginning of the month.

Each recipe is delicious and passes the Sunday Dinner Test of a centre piece main dish looking good on the table, surrounded by dishes of vegetables. A visual treat as well as a memorable meal.

## Land of Hope and Glory on your plate

I describe these dishes as Sunday Dinner because in my youth there were only two possible meals on a Sunday: dinner, and tea. The best Sunday meals are eaten mid-afternoon, starting around 3 o'clock, and ending at about 6. 'Tea' would be a snack much later. Sunday is special and leisurely. You will probably have a starter, of course, and a pudding or two. I will leave those courses up to you, though I will make a suggestion, to get your imagination working. Traditionally, Yorkshire pudding with gravy was served as a starter! In Yorkshire of course, this idea has all but died out, how about bringing it back? A small light omelette makes a very good and unusual first course before roast lamb and is quite normal in France. For a pudding, after the large meal of roast meat, why not try something light such as lemon tart, or a simple baked apple, or pears in red wine? Let your imagination lead you down unexpected paths! Similarly, I'll leave it to you to decide on the vegetables. Roast potatoes are probably a must, with parsnips or carrots maybe. I will suggest a couple of more unusual vegetables along the way.

Roast Beef is of course the classic English dinner. We shouldn't forget that food has played a huge part in both our history and in shaping our national identity. It is enshrined in our heritage. Roast beef is as English as conkers, warm beer, Agincourt, and cricket! It is "Land of Hope and Glory" on your plate. In the 17th and 18th Centuries, roast beef became such a fashionable way of showing the national identity in a world of change and revolution, that clubs and societies were founded, such as the "Beefsteak Club" and "The Sublime Society of Beefsteaks". The motto of the Beefsteak Club was 'Beef and Liberty!' Remember that the Yeoman Warders at the Tower of London, are forever known colloquially as 'Beefeaters'!

The sea shanty "The Roast Beef of Olde England" was written around 1735, and was designed to stir up animosity between the French and the English. The writer compares the ragout eating French with the sturdy John Bull who defeated the Spanish Armada on a diet of roast beef, and he berates the English for sliding towards effeminate 'continental' ways!

The artist William Hogarth, a member of The

Beefsteak Club, painted a picture which was also called "The Roast Beef of Olde England", in which he depicts an Englishman at the gates of Calais carrying a huge side of beef, and the French as a scrawny rabble existing on watery soup! Of course, foreigners sneered at English cooking, saying we could only cook roast beef and plum pudding! The old rivalries are still with us, the French have long called the English 'lesrosbifs' or 'les biftecks'.

But then they have berets and snails!

## And so to buying your meat

I find a real butcher will provide a more flexible range of cuts than a supermarket. A real butcher is not necessarily more expensive. I bought all the meat for my recipes from Harty Meats, they operate on the Burden family farm at Old Rides Farm, Eastchurch, Isle of Sheppey located on the Isle of Harty in Kent.

So far they only open their tiny shop Friday to Sunday each week. The walls are decorated with rosettes and certificates they have won for their livestock. All their beef and lamb comes from the Burden family farm, they source their pork from another local farm in Stockbury.

I think it is always better to buy your meat from a source where they take pride and care, loving care even, in how they rear their animals. During the season they sell game of all kinds, and wild rabbits. The butcher, (pictured above) Chris, is very helpful and full of advice. He's never in a hurry, so feel free to ask his advice. Standing there watching Chris heft another whole pig into the shop and proceed to expertly and quickly cut for me my relatively cheap order made me think that visiting a butcher like this is about as far removed from buying meat in a supermarket as you can get, and all the better for that!

There are places like this all over the country if you look and ask!

## Now a few rules

Always make sure your meat is at room temperature, don't take it straight from the fridge to the oven.

Always heat a little oil or dripping in a roasting tin and seal the meat on all sides before seasoning with salt, because salt draws out the juices from the meat and you want to keep them inside! Always have a preheated oven. Cook meat for 20 minutes in a hot oven, 200°C (400°F, gas 6), then reduce the heat to 160°C (325°F, gas 3) for further cooking.

Timing is usually calculated: 15 minutes for every 450g (1lb) of the meat, plus another 20 minutes. Test by pushing askewer into the largest section of the meat. Judge how well it is cooked by the colour of the juices that run out.

When your meat is cooked, always let it rest for a while, maybe 15 to 20 minutes before carving and serving. Simply remove from the oven and cover with a clean tea towel while you make the gravy or finish the vegetables.

# Lamb in an orchard

Serves 6

This is my version of a Crown Roast. Early in the Twentieth Century, the crown roast was thought of as the epitome of an elegant dinner party. A row of about 12 end of neck lamb chops circled to represent a crown, with little paper crowns on the tip of each chop bone. Sadly, this tasty honest dish has fallen out of favour, nowadays being associated with a certain type of hotel or restaurant that pretends to the sort of grandness that it cannot deliver, which is a shame, because it has almost disappeared from the culinary landscape. This is not a cut of lamb that you will find in a supermarket. Even your local butcher may require some notice in order to prepare it. Luckily, my butcher wasn't disconcerted by my request and we discussed what I wanted, I demonstrated with my fingers, "like this, like an avenue of trees bending towards each other". "I get you, a 'guard of honour'", he replied, a gleam in his eye. And he did, 10 minutes later I left the shop. That's what I call service.

**Lamb chops, estimate 2 or 3 chops per person, best end of neck, in 2 'rows' (mine weighed 1.75 kg/1lb 80z)**
**2 tbs honey**
**2 tbs mint sauce combined with the juice of half an orange**
**3 Russet apples, cored and chopped**
**2 heads of garlic, halved**
**Rosemary**
**Fresh pepper and salt**

### METHOD
Rub the lamb with the honey, mint sauce and orange. Arrange the two racks of chops so that the bones interlock and cross over, forming an avenue. Tie together at 3 points. Cover the tips of each bone with tin foil, this stop the ends burning. Into the space between the two racks of chops, slide in the garlic, the chopped apple and a length of fresh rosemary. Season with pepper, and roast as before in an oven at 180°C (350°F, gas 4). When cooked, remove from the oven and allow to rest, using the time to make the gravy. Remove the tin foil caps from the ends of the chops. Actually the gravy will have made itself! Serve, spectacularly, perhaps with mashed root vegetables. And don't you dare put any of those little paper hats on the bones!

# Be my Valentine!

Men, take note: **Clarissa Porter** suggests you don't take your loved one out to a busy restaurant, but rather entertain her at home, in style

**T**ry and book a restaurant in my neck of the woods for February 14th. Maybe, if you book in December three months ahead, you will be successful, otherwise no hope. But I think it's an unfortunate trend that Valentine's Day is now heavily dependent on a restaurant meal for the loving couple. That's a long way from the origins of this unique day, which is more like legend than fact, with no one really knowing for sure if it is true.

It seems that in Ancient Rome, there was a Christian priest called Valentine. The Emperor was Claudius the 2nd. Not the cuddly stuttering Claudius from the TV series, but a later Emperor also known as Claudius the Goth, or Claudius the Terrible. Emperor Claudius was always waging war somewhere, so he needed a never ending supply of young men for his armies.

The Romans had a form of conscription, but it was possible to evade being forced to "join up" if you were married. So, Claudius, his supply of young men dwindling, forbade the practise of the Christian marriage. The story goes that Valentine continued marrying young couples in secret, and then when he was found out, he was imprisoned and subsequently beheaded for disobeying Claudius. There is another story that while he was in prison his jailer's daughter was kind to him, and on the day of his execution he sent her a yellow crocus with a note which said: "Remember your Valentine". He was reputedly executed on February 14th. I should say that the Vatican has disowned Valentine as a saint, so they have doubts about the authenticity of this legend.

What is true however, is that 'February' is derived from Latin, and is connected with the Ancient Roman festival of Lupercalia, which began on February 15th. The Lupercalia was a festival of fertility and purification, which took place just after the beginning of the Roman Spring on February 5th. On February 15th, goats were sacrificed, and young men wearing nothing but goatskins ran around a sacred site, the Palatine hill. The Palatine contained the cave where Romulus and Remus were suckled by a she-wolf, the cave was known as the Lupercal.

Young women watching the young men running, were struck with strips of goat skin, known as februa, to promote fertility. Ovid wrote, "submit with patience to the blows dealt by a fruitful hand." The origins of this festival are the origins of Rome itself.

Therefore, I think it is reasonable to suppose that as with other seasonal festivals, the early Christian church accommodated the Lupercalia, and ultimately subdued it, by judicious promotion of the legend of St Valentine.

## Back to the present day!

Valentine's Day has become hugely commercial. Rather than spend a fortune crammed into an overbooked and over-stretched restaurant with dozens of other couples, why not cook an edible Valentine's card? Something simple yet romantic and homely.

I would be very impressed if the man in my life took the time and a little trouble to rustle up one or two of these dishes for our Valentine meal, and I'd rather be alone with him than in a crowded restaurant! ●

# Creamy cheese heart with fruity sauce

Serves 2 (or more)

This is so easy to make and looks really stunning and unusual. You will need a china 'creme a la coeur' mould, either a large one, or four small ones. These are heart shaped moulds, perforated on the underneath. They are easy to find in cookware stores. Preferably you should make this the day before and leave in a fridge overnight. But you can make it the same day if you like.

**3 250g (9oz) tubs of ricotta cheese**
**6 tbs caster or icing sugar**
**2 tsp almond essence**
**zest of a lime**
**juice of half a lime**
**small tub of double cream**
**small piece of muslin to line your mould**
**1 packet of frozen mixed berries (supermarkets stock these)**
**dash of Kirsch, or a little mint**
**sugar to taste**

**METHOD**

Beat together the cheese, sugar and almond essence until you have a smooth mixture. Then fold in the cream, add the zest and the lime juice. Line your mould with clean muslin. Spoon in the mixture and then place the mould on a plate and put it in the fridge.

To make the sauce, gently warm the berries and sugar until the sugar dissolves. Add either a dash of Kirsch or a sprig of fresh mint, and allow to cool. When you are ready to serve, place your serving plate over the mould and invert so that the creamy heart is transferred to the plate. Carefully peel off the muslin. Serve the heart surrounded by some of the sauce, and have some sauce available to serve separately.

Serves 2

You've guessed it, bread and cheese! But really rather special bread and cheese, just right after a long romantic walk in the woods on Valentine's Day!

**For the bread**
**60g (2½oz) butter**
**1 dsp sugar**
**290ml (½pt) beer**
**30g (1¼oz) fresh yeast**
**1 tsp salt**
**1 egg beaten**
**555g (1lb 4oz) whole-wheat flour, sieved**
**60g (2½oz) walnut pieces, not too big!**

## METHOD
Grease a baking tray. Put the ale and the butter in a saucepan and bring to the boil. Allow to cool till lukewarm. Mix the yeast with a little of the beer mixture. Then add the sugar, salt and egg to the yeast. Sift the flour into a large bowl. Pour in the beer and yeast mixtures and mix together first with a knife, and then with your hands. Knead for about 10 minutes until smooth and shiny. Cover with a clean tea towel and leave somewhere warm until the dough has doubled in size. Knead again and scatter in the walnut pieces.

Shape the dough into a heart and place on the baking tray. Leave in a warm place until the dough rises again (this is the size the bread will be when it is baked).

Place in a preheated oven at 200°C (400°F, gas 6) for 35 minutes. Remove and place on a wire rack to cool. You can test to see if it is cooked by tapping on the underside, it should sound hollow!

## For the potted Stilton

**225g (8oz) Stilton cheese**
**55g (2oz) butter**
**pinch of mace**
**½ tsp English mustard**
**Few walnuts for garnish**

## METHOD
Crumble the cheese and work in the butter, mace, and mustard. Place in a suitable mould or ramekin. I used a heart shaped ramekin by *Le Creuset*. As an alternative to the mace and mustard, you could add 2 tablespoons of port or sherry. Serve with the bread still warm so that the cheese almost melts into the bread.

# Beer and walnut bread with potted Stilton